IN YOUR OWN
BACKYARD

IN YOUR OWN BACKYARD

How to Create and Enjoy
Your Own Private Retreat

Written and illustrated by
A. Cort Sinnes

Andrews and McMeel

Published in 1992 in the United States of America by
Andrews and McMeel
a Universal Press Syndicate Company
4900 Main Street
Kansas City, Missouri 64112

This book was designed and produced by
Hearth & Garden Productions
A. Cort Sinnes, Designer
Christine Beyer, Production Manager
Copy Editors: Katie Lazar, Mary Harrison
Line Art: Peter Ruhl
Photography: Bruce Bandle, Amberlight Photography

The author would like to thank the following publishers and authors for permission to include excerpts from their books:
Celebrations: The Complete Book of American Holidays, written by Robert Myers with the editors of Hallmark Cards. Published by Doubleday, 1972.
The Education of a Gardener, written by Russell Page. Copyright © 1962, 1983 by Russell Page. Published by Random House.
David Hicks Garden Design, by David Hicks. Copyright © 1982 by David Hicks. Published by Routledge & Kegan Paul Ltd.
The Amateur Naturalist, written by Gerald Durrell. Copyright © 1982 by Dorling Kindersley Limited, London. Text Copyright © 1982 by Gerald Durrell. Published by Alfred A. Knopf, Inc.

For Virginia and Sarah,
the "sister women,"
whose own backyard is a world unto itself,
brimming over with earthly delights.

Acknowledgments

To Katie and Brooke, who had the foresight and wisdom to leave their own backyard during the final push to the deadline. Thanks for your support and love; you can come home now.

To my parents, for letting me loose in their own backyard and giving me the space and freedom to explore.

To Gene, Lucille, Mary Jane, Pete, and Louis of Van Winden's Nursery, who shared so freely of their considerable wisdom with a teenager who definitely learned while he earned.

To the late Walter Doty, a world-class teacher, mentor, unabashed genius, and crank, who took one more "stooge" under his wing and taught him what it was like to fly with an idea.

To Harriet Choice, this writer's editor-come-true, who had the vision to put down her fork and say "that's it!," when all I said was "backyard."

To Kathy Andrews, Tom Thornton, Donna Martin, George Diggs, Elizabeth Andersen, and Alan McDermott of Universal Press Syndicate and Andrews and McMeel, for being part of an organization that respects the written word, those who write them, and for remaining unflaggingly principled in a world that sometimes seems to have left such concepts behind.

To Chuck Rubin, for promoting, protecting, and *pro bono* advice. You're the best.

To Christine Beyer, for her enthusiasm, support, technical expertise, and willing spirit, especially during the dog days.

To Pete Ruhl, "the professor," for his good-natured help in the drawing department, especially his assistance in getting my "Thots" worked out.

To Jim Stockton, for his wise counsel and good choice of restaurants.

All of you helped grow this project. Without your help and support, this book would not exist. Thank you.

CONTENTS

	Prologue	x
I	Private Possibilities	13
II	From Vapor to Paper—and Beyond	19
III	Backyard Building	29
IV	Planting the Plan	45
V	"God Is in the Details"	59
VI	Backyard Celebrations	71
VII	Backyard Games	85
VIII	Backyard Meals	95
IX	Backyard Kids	103
X	Backyard Naturalist	111
	Epilogue	121
	Product Index	122
	Product Sources	123
	Index	124

PROLOGUE

I keep telling them we need to have more fun. Everyone always seems so busy and worried and stuff. When we're outside, it's not like that. So I try to get them to do things like eat outside.

"Hey, Mom, can we eat outside?"

"I don't know, let me think about it."

"I'll carry the stuff out."

"Okay."

Eating outdoors is fun. You can spill a whole glass of milk on the lawn and nobody will yell at you. You can jump up from the table to catch a firefly and none of the adults will give you a dirty look because they're too busy having fun, too. Being outside is easy. I never go inside unless I have to.

I like yards with big lawns. Lawns that get watered in the evening with those Rainbird sprinklers—"chit, chit, chit, chit, chiiiiiiiit"—back and forth. I like the way the sun, just before it sets, cuts between the top of the fence and the bottom of the leaves, making long shadows across the lawn and turning each drop of water into a shining, twirling crystal, hurling towards the ground.

If you leave the sprinkler on too long, the lawn squishes between your toes. You should always go barefoot in backyards, even when you're climbing a tree, spying on your neighbor.

My father and I built a tree fort in a pear tree—a tree platform, really. It's got a rope ladder that you can pull up after you're in the fort. Sometimes my friend and I use the tree fort for throwing rotten pears at our other friends. It's also a great place to launch water balloons and airplanes. I sit up there and read a lot. My friend has to yell at me from the ground to let the rope ladder down.

Backyards are great at nighttime. Especially if your parents let you sleep out on the lawn. We make tents from old sheets and clothespins. I like waking up in the middle of the night and walking around the yard. After the moon has set, the stars are so bright it's like walking in space. I like the way the sleeping bag and sheets smell the next morning when they're wet with dew.

I help take care of the garden. My father plants a vegetable garden every year. After he's through planting the seeds he crouches over and starts doing a strut and hoots with his hand over his mouth. He says it's an Old Country custom. I don't know what old country he's talking about, but he never acts like that indoors.

I mow the lawn every week. I go over it twice, each time in opposite directions. It makes a checkerboard pattern. People say we have the prettiest yard in the neighborhood. Other people ask me to take care of their lawns for them. The old ladies pay more than the men, and they're almost always home after I finish mowing the lawn. Sometimes they invite me in for cookies or some hard candy. They always seem to have that candy sitting on their coffee tables in some kind of fancy glass dish. If they're not home, they leave the money in the mailbox in an envelope with my name on it.

This summer we had a carnival in my friend's backyard. Four of us put it on. We had food to eat, games to play, and weird things to look at, like Mr. Kelso's false teeth that he put in the wet concrete while they were building his patio. We had a big jar full of beans. You had to try and guess how many beans were in there. It cost 10¢ a try. My friend's mom was the one who counted out the 10,023 beans. It took her a whole night. We made posters to announce the carnival and tied them to our backs. Then we rode our bicycles around the neighborhood yelling. Everybody came. We made enough money for all four of us to go to the movies and have extra stuff to eat. We're going to do the carnival every summer.

Last year at Halloween my parents let me have a party. They planned some games for me and my friends. Then they turned out the lights in our basement and lit a candle. My mom read this weird poem about an old dead man and we had to pass around stuff like peeled grapes and liver. Everyone screamed their heads off. After that my mom led us into the backyard. It was already dark and cold. She said maybe we would be able to see the old man's ghost. Everyone was bumping into everyone else and kind of holding on to each others' costumes. It was a little scary in the dark. All of the sudden, this big white thing flew up right next to us and into the tree. Everyone screamed and ran all over the place. My best friend ran home and didn't come back. He didn't come to school the next day, either. Later, my dad told me the ghost was just a sheet over basketball that he threw up into the tree. He never acts like that indoors.

I'm never going inside unless I have to.

A.C.S.
Summer, 1964

A cup of coffee, the comics, and a sunny Sunday in your own backyard. What more could you ask for— except, perhaps, a push on the swing.

PRIVATE POSSIBILITIES

lthough a lifetime of experience has gone into this book, it didn't really start to take shape until about twelve years ago. The "green-eyed monster," jealousy, played a part, I think. My wife and I were living in a second-floor flat, and for the first time in our lives did not have a backyard to call our own. Early one Sunday morning, as we sat down to breakfast, I caught sight of our next-door neighbors. They were sitting very comfortably in a pair of old wicker chairs set up on the lawn in their backyard. There was a fat Sunday newspaper and a stack of magazines next to the chairs, a small table set up for serving coffee in two big mugs, and something to snack on for breakfast, all close at hand. A child sat in a swing, calling for a push. A big orange and white cat rolled over in a patch of sunlit grass. Birds sang excitedly to each other from overhanging trees.

It was a small, peaceful world, contained in a neighborhood that was gingerly shaking itself awake. I had trouble looking away, admiring the privacy of the scene while at the same time invading it. There *they* were, out in that green retreat—all leafy beauty and dappled sunlight—and there *we* were, indoors, in a stuffy kitchen, with the radio, television, and telephone far too close at hand, looking longingly out the window. Never again, we vowed, would we be without a backyard.

Years later, as the editor of a national gardening magazine, I had the opportunity to peek (legitimately this time) into many other backyards all over the country. I learned

"If that Sunday paper gets any heavier, I'm leaving it on the front lawn."

that the common denominator in the most satisfying backyards was a sense of enclosure and protection—exactly the conditions of the Sunday morning scene I had coveted years earlier. Privacy, it seemed, was at the heart of the best-loved backyards.

Whether you use the backyard as a place to play, take a meal or a nap, build a fort or tend a garden, this secluded outdoor place naturally leads to homespun diversions. Humble as they may be, these simple pleasures, a little peace, and the time to enjoy them richly add to the sum of our private lives.

Personal Pursuits

As much as any room inside the house, and certainly more than your front yard, a backyard can be a space for self-expression, any way you care to express it. Remember, it's *your* backyard.

To this day, I have no idea what led my friend's father, as noted in the prologue, to embed those sets of false teeth and marbles in the still-wet concrete of his new patio. Because he made false teeth for a living, he may have seen them as a kind of heraldic emblem, or perhaps as a sign indicating his guild (although this *still* doesn't explain the marbles). Whatever those false choppers represented, they enchanted all of the kids in the neighborhood, and certainly left a lasting impression on me. If there was a lesson to be learned, it had something to do with seeing a backyard as a playful place—a place where adults might surprise kids and act like kids themselves.

Both goldfish and koi are quick to respond to the hand that feeds them. Long-lived and requiring little care, they may be the perfect pet.

So please don't be misled into thinking that the tree house your kids want so badly is going to somehow ruin the English-cottage-garden look you desire. Backyards are forgiving places. They are places where *life* happens, not a set piece or a backdrop for an advertisement in a magazine. You'll have a lot more fun if you relax a little and leave any strict notion of bad taste on the back porch.

Grandpa's Private Playground

Some people take to creating a backyard the way Picasso took to a blank canvas. With a full head of inspiration and virtually no hesitation, these backyard virtuosos shape and plant their plot of land like a person possessed, which, in a way, they are. At some point, the seed of an idea dropped in their fertile imaginations and nothing, it seems, can stand in the way of their efforts to make it a reality. The results these people achieve stand as testimonies to what any backyard can become, given enough energy, time, and materials.

One of my favorite backyards is owned by a respected lawyer and young grandfather. His suburban backyard exemplifies everything that a backyard can be, sometimes to the consternation of his wife, who now hesitates to leave home for more than a week at a time, for fear of what he'll do next. Be that as it may, this private haven delights both family and friends, especially those visiting grandchildren, who call it "Grandpa's private playground." While his backyard is not what would be called grand in size, it is certainly grand in spirit. In a space approximately 60 by 150 feet, he has shoehorned a swimming pool, a grass sport court (regulation-sized, for badminton and volleyball, and on which many a multigenerational game has been played), and a specially designed deck where he, his wife, and their friends stage one-act plays. New this year is a waterfall and a fish pond stocked with koi. My friend was delighted that, after just a couple of months, the koi had learned to eat from his hand. With two comfortable wooden benches on either side of the pond, this has become his favorite spot to sit at the end of the day, enjoying a sundowner, admiring the brilliantly colored koi as they fluidly appear and disappear in the dark water.

As for gardening, there's a collection of scented geraniums displayed on a wrought iron baker's rack, a few large containers filled with flowering annuals, the lawn, and a row of mature shade trees across the back of the lot. His wife tends a few pots planted with herbs next to the kitchen door. As attractive as it is, there is little upkeep. Although he spends the majority of his free time in his backyard, he spends only about an hour or so each week gardening. He sometimes thinks about getting a smaller place, a condominium or some such thing, but says he can't bear the thought of giving up his backyard.

The Backyard Express

Another backyard I frequently visit is a playground of a different stripe. A large section of ground, completely encircling the patio, has been given over to a model train set-up, landscaped in miniature, complete with tunnels, trestles, and railroad crossings. A passion such as this obviously takes plenty of upkeep ("high maintenance, but worth it," according to the owner). The biggest problem to date has been in keeping the family cats from fouling the tracks; it seems they're attracted to the gravel road bed.

Where the Wild Things Grow

Then there's the blithe spirit who has let his backyard return to the wild, content to lay down a fresh path of bark chips every year or so, just so he can find his way from one end of this urban forest to the other. Volunteer trees have been left to grow where they will, weeds and wildflowers tumble over one another in abandon, and if there ever was a lawn, it has long since been overgrown. "The kids in the neighborhood

A Long-standing Compromise

For as long as there have been American neighborhoods, front yards have been viewed differently from backyards. In 1917 Frances Duncan wrote a practical and spirited book of advice to "surburban" homeowners titled, The Joyous Art of Gardening. Although the book, unfortunately, is long out-of-print, Duncan's observations are still fresh and valid. In it, Duncan gives the following advice concerning the split personalities of front and backyards:

"The simplest way of meeting most of the difficulty of the street and the neighbor is to compromise—to divide the grounds to the 'street side' and the 'garden side'; to 'rend unto Caesar the things that are Caesar's,' and on the street side plant to promote the general welfare, so that the house may with some degree of grace take its place among its fellows, while at the back of the house one may cheerfully engage in the pursuit of individual happiness and, planting after the imaginations of his heart, make his garden to suit himself."

"The easiest way around that cat problem would be to just get rid of the cats...or get a much bigger train."

IT'S YOUR YARD.
DO WHAT YOU WANT TO DO

FOR THOSE WITH A BENT FOR THINGS THESPIAN, A DECK CAN EASILY BE TRANSFORMED INTO AN IMPROMPTU STAGE.

YOUR OWN PRIVATE CROQUET COURT, PLANTED WITH BENTGRASS? WHY NOT?

DEFINITELY A FLIGHT OF FANCY, THIS TREE HOUSE IS SURE TO MAKE YOUR BACKYARD A POPULAR SPOT. DON'T FORGET TO LET THE KIDS DOWN!

VERY POPULAR IN EUROPE, AND GAINING GROUND HERE, ARE OUTDOOR MODEL TRAIN INSTALLATIONS. JUST BE SURE THE CONDUCTOR KEEPS AN EYE OUT FOR OBSTRUCTIONS ON THE TRACK.

THERE ARE FEW "MUST-HAVES" IN ANY BACKYARD, BUT A SWING SURE COMES CLOSE.

treat this wild place as their personal playground," he says. "Every bird, squirrel, bee, and butterfly thinks it is home. It's not neat, like most other backyards, but its wildness sort of excites the imagination of the kids."

Of course, the tree house he designed in a wild state of his own is a big draw, too. Looking something like a hanging gazebo, this flight of fancy is attached to a massive rope, threaded through a massive pulley, which is attached to an even more massive limb. The kids climb in, close the screen door, and then are hoisted into the upper reaches of a leafy and private realm. The only requirement for this suspended fun is the presence of three or four strong adults to pull the "sky-fort" into the air.

Crazy for Bentgrass

In another neighborhood, not far from where the wild things grow, lives a family who became so involved with croquet that they were possessed with the idea of planting a fine-bladed, bentgrass lawn in an area of the country where everyone told them bentgrass wouldn't grow. After excavating the soil to a depth of a foot or so, and filling it with tons of sand for perfect drainage, five years later the bentgrass continues to thrive in their backyard and the crack of croquet mallets echoes long into the summer nights.

To Swing on a Star

Last, but hardly least, was the woman who wanted nothing more of a backyard than a large lawn and a larger tree—but the tree had to have just the right branch from which to hang an old-fashioned swing. In fact, the right combination of house, backyard, and tree became a priority when house-hunting. Once found, the owner seems forever content. "I don't know if I can explain it, " she said, "but there's something about swinging that takes me back to my childhood. It's great to be able to provide the same, simple pleasure for my own kids, but even better when no one is around, and I have the swing to myself."

Benign Obsessions

When I was a child, my parents would drive past a particular country estate every year on the way to our summer place. At a certain turn in the road, I remember pleading with them to slow down so I could take in the details of a rather fantastic scene, especially for the foothills of northern California. This was not your typical backyard, by any means. To the side of the house, the owners had dug a very large pond. In the middle of the pond was a small island, probably 20 by 30 feet, with a bright red Chinese pavilion, surrounded by fledgling weeping willows. One year, I noticed a sampan drawn up to the island, but by then the willows had grown so large that I couldn't see what might be happening in the pavilion, which is probably just as the owners intended. It had the power, however, to excite the imagination of one 11-year-old for many years to come.

Somewhere between that red Chinese pavilion on a private pond and those false teeth in my friend's patio, I realized early on that backyards were places where fantasies could be made real. These fantasies were seldom within the bounds of what was currently fashionable nor, nine times out of ten, were they any more "appropriate" than a model train chugging around a patio, a swinging treehouse, or a bentgrass lawn in the Midwest. Each contained an element of delightful defiance: "Yes, I know this probably shouldn't or can't be done, but I'm going to do it anyway, just for the sheer fun of it."

Obsessions? Probably. But of the most benign and satisfying sort.

Two Masters Speak

Two world-class garden designers, the late Thomas Church and the late Russell Page, observed an important change in their clients' attitudes after the end of World War II. Today it may seem natural to think less about gardening and more about outdoor living, but when the shift in emphasis began, it appeared quite revolutionary.

In his book, Your Private World, *Thomas Church wrote: "Western living created one kind of revolution, and the garden became as much a year-round living environment as the house…The only trend we can see is a trend away from trends. People are worrying less about fashion in homes and landscapes and more about what pleases them and serves the needs of their family best."*

From Russell Page's book, The Education of a Gardener: *"We might now consider the small garden where horticulture takes second place to the pleasures and needs of out-of-door living.*

"In the climates of California, Texas, and Arizona…a new garden form is evolving whose pattern is moving eastwards towards Europe and south towards the Latin Americas. This formula or theme is based on the admission that space for car-parking, the swimming pool and its surround, the children's playground, the out-of-door dining-room and kitchen, and the potting-shed and salad-ground, may take up perhaps three quarters of the area. The new tendency is no longer to consider them as necessities infringing on precious garden space but as a form of gardening or, if you prefer it, landscaping."

"Garden, landscape, backyard…call it what you like, just as long as there are a few trees."

*Once the bug bites to do
something with your
backyard, it's hard to
resist the temptation of
just starting in blindly.
The most satisfying
results, however, are the
product of many hours of
simply contemplating
the possibilities.*

FROM VAPOR TO PAPER—
AND BEYOND

 sunny spring morning finds you sitting on the back steps, soaking up the sun. You think to yourself how pleasant it is just to be outdoors. With that thought in mind, you take a long look at your backyard and begin to wonder: "Isn't there something that can be done to make this place a little more…" what? Livable? Attractive? With a place to eat outdoors? Or a place to let a toddler roam free?

The desire to fix up your backyard may become so strong that you firmly resolve to do something about it, immediately. Unfortunately, you halt on the next step, because you're not sure what *it* should be. If you're like most people, you go back indoors, disappointedly dragging a half-hearted resolution to start on the project some other day.

Take heart. The fact is, you've already started fixing up your backyard by simply looking at it. The best backyards develop from many hours of this seemingly passive activity— just sitting and imagining how one idea or another might look.

In retrospect you'll see the value in taking your time, because your first ideas are seldom the best. And rushing in before you really know what you want, or how to do it, could result in costly mistakes. A backyard is a changeable place, one way in spring or summer, and quite another in fall or winter. Your *ideas* will change (and probably improve) over a period of time, too. If you sit there and look at it with an open mind from one season to the next, you'll be surprised at the good ideas that will eventually evolve.

"What's the big deal? Just get out there, dig a few holes and throw some dirt around. That's my advice."

19

Plan or No Plan?

There are people who, once they have their ideas in mind, find it easy to plan an entire backyard, right down to where the hammock will be placed, all in their heads or on the back of the proverbial cocktail napkin. The only question one could ask of these creative souls is "What are you waiting for?"

And then there are the less-gifted (but no less inspired) types who, although their backyards would benefit from the process of making a plan on paper, refuse to do so. They find themselves overcome by the need to do something—*anything*—to improve their backyard and simply start in. Their idea of what needs to be done usually involves mowing an overgrown lawn, hacking away at some brutish weeds, and finally, as a reward, taking a trip to the local nursery or garden center. Once home, with the plants that caught their eye in the nursery firmly planted in the ground, no-plan people are usually not quite sure what they've done, but content with the fact that at least they've done something.

This is risky business on two counts. First, plants purchased on impulse rarely wind up in a location that's best for them. Second, if you're interested in a backyard as a living space for people, plants are one of the last things you add.

If this scenario sounds all too familiar, don't think you're the only one who's confused. When it comes to backyards, the most common mistake is confusing the planting process with the process of creating an outdoor living space for people. Although plants definitely help, they are only one component in creating a satisfying backyard. Without a plan, one spontaneous spurt of action is usually followed by another, right up to the almost inevitable, unsatisfactory conclusion: a backyard that satisfies neither plants nor people.

Plan or no plan? Only you can answer the question. The objective on the following pages is for you to develop some clear ideas of what you want your backyard to provide and how you want it to look—specifically. This will lead to a plan on paper, which will help you or someone you hire make sure those ideas take shape in reality.

For those of you who haven't done a thing yet except sit and look at your backyard, you've already done the best thing you can do to get started. The next step is to get up off the stoop and walk around, but that's getting ahead of the story. Before walking around your yard, it may be important to walk backwards—through time—to find a few of the things that could be important in creating your own personal retreat.

The Vapor Stage

Virtually everyone remembers an outdoor place, either real or imagined, that deeply satisfied them as a child. It may have been an elderly neighbor's flower garden, with dahlias as big as your head, three-foot-tall marigolds, and trailing nasturtiums that nearly covered the paths. Or it may have been farther afield, like that shady, cool grove of trees at summer camp where cookouts were held. Perhaps it was your uncle's vegetable garden, where you had your first taste of a warm, sun-ripened tomato right off the vine (made so much more intriguing when that tiny shaker of salt appeared like magic from behind a stone bench). Or that fort you made from scrap lumber, which seemed like the neatest place in the world because it was *yours,* and you helped build it.

Any backyard holds the potential to satisfy you in the same way as any of those early outdoor experiences. The first step in creating a satisfying place, however, is to identify, as clearly as you can, what it was that appealed to you. Pull a lounge chair out onto the porch or under a shady tree and ask yourself: What was it about that old neighbor's flower garden that was so compelling? Was it a jumble of plants, one tumbling over the other, an almost wild scene of color and fragrance, like walking into a domestic jungle—perhaps just the opposite of your parents' tidy yard? What made that fort so great? The feeling of enclosure, of being able to see out but not to be seen? Or the fact that everything you needed for comfort and protection was close at hand? And that vegetable garden—was it simply the fact that food was growing right before your eyes that made it so attractive? Or was it the sensual delight of being able to let the juice of the tomato dribble right over your bare tummy without being told it wasn't a proper thing to do?

There's no need to write down these thoughts and feelings, but it is important to bear them in mind throughout each stage of the following process. Trust your instincts and be willing to modify your plan, even if the only reason you can give for doing so is because "it just doesn't feel right." In the pragmatic world of committing plans to paper, the list of instructions rarely includes "follow your heart"; when it comes to backyards, perhaps it should be added, right up there near the top.

Bear in mind Thomas Wolfe's caveat, namely, that "you can't go home again." Of course, he was right: you can't. The point of digging in the past is not to duplicate some childhood memory, but to identify the way those places made you *feel*. It's no accident that the most satisfying backyards are born from a childlike imagination and devil-may-care vitality. Just beneath the surface of many adults who have created great backyards is a kid who couldn't wait to get out there and play in the dirt.

The Paper Stage

At this stage in the backyard planning process we move from the past to the present. Here are the supplies to assemble:

1) A binder
2) Approximately 200 sheets of binder paper
3) Scissors
4) Several sharp pencils, with good erasers
5) Tape
6) Ruler
7) A few sheets of standard graph paper

Filching Ideas

"Filching" may be too strong a word. How about "permanently borrowing"? No matter which word you use, picking up ideas from one place or another is one of the important ways any backyard develops. Every time you visit a friend's backyard, walk through a public garden, or have the opportunity to peek into a stranger's yard, keep your eyes open for ideas you can steal…um, borrow.

David Hicks is an internationally known and universally respected garden designer. He travels a great deal, and often returns home with his head full of ideas collected from around the world. Here's some sound advice from his excellent book, David Hicks Garden Design: *"…when looking at a garden, discard those elements which are of no interest to you: concentrate your senses and your analysis on those things which appeal. Test them—do you like them enough to want to adapt or modify them for your garden? If not, forget them. If they pass the test, assess them in detail—see how they work, and how they could be made to work for you." If you're traveling and have your camera handy, take a photograph of the thing that catches your eye. It's one of the best ways to remember details.*

Although it may seem to be a contradiction, borrowing ideas from other places often leads to the most personable of backyards. No one else would put those ideas together in exactly the same way as you, and no one else would have modified them in the same way. In the end, this collection of borrowed ideas will result in a unique expression of your own experiences and vision.

"I'd like to be there when he goes through customs with a headful of those purloined ideas."

With the above materials, and an armful of home and garden magazines, the object is to create your personal backyard scrapbook. This may sound rather sophomoric, but it's the best thing you can do to ensure that your backyard turns out the way you want it. The scrapbook will be invaluable on trips to the nursery, hardware store, or lumberyard, and it will help to avoid disappointments when dealing with contractors, carpenters, bricklayers, concrete masons, and landscapers.

When you hear the bellicose command, "Show me, don't tell me," instead of waving your hands in the air and hoping for the best, point to the exact thing you want: "I want this pattern picket for the fence, with this type of finial on the posts, the whole thing painted white, with a gate exactly like this, with this—right here—this set of hinges and that type of latch." In their defense, contractors and tradespeople are put in a difficult position when they are expected to make real what they *think* is in the client's mind. So do everyone a favor: Assemble a backyard scrapbook before the first shovelful of earth is turned.

Pick a quiet time to go through the magazines, and look at them slowly and deliberately. Carefully search the corners of each photograph to see if anything catches your eye. It might be something as simple as the handle on a gate, a piece of outdoor furniture, the shape of a deck, or the color of a fence. No detail is insignificant.

Each time you see something appealing in a photograph or illustration, cut the picture out of the magazine and tape it to a piece of binder paper. Be sure to make notations on the paper as to what it is, specifically, that you like. Three months later, in an entirely different frame of mind, you may find

Everything you need to create your own backyard scrapbook: 1) a binder, 2) scissors, 3) paper, 4) tape, 5) a ruler, 6) some sharp pencils and, hopefully, 7) a good idea or two.

yourself wondering what it was in the photograph that caught your eye.

At this stage, there's no real need to organize the scrapbook. It's enough just to make sure that the pages get put into the binder so they won't get scattered to the wind. There will be plenty of time to organize the images later.

Depending on the sense of urgency, the scrapbook can be assembled over a long weekend, over a few months, or slowly over a period of years. This is a process that benefits from a leisurely approach, allowing for changes in needs, tastes, and desires. If, however, you have a specific deadline or timetable—like "this is the year we're going to fix up the backyard, and we're going to finish it before we leave on vacation"— look at as many magazines as you can get your hands on to see the widest possible range of ideas.

Taking Your Ideas Public

Unless you live by yourself, or are the "dictator of design" in your household, there's going to come a time when you must take your ideas public. If there are kids in the household, the route you take largely depends on how old they are. Under seven or eight years old, they will probably go along lovingly and support any ideas you might have, especially if the plans include some things specifically for them. Once children reach the age of nine or ten, they have their own rather well-defined priorities and ideas.

Before implementing any plan, it may behoove you to make sure everyone's needs are being met. The best possible scenario involves a meeting of all members of the household, resulting in great ideas you, on your own, would never have come up with. Even in this decidedly democratic exercise, it's a good idea if one person runs the show. Otherwise, the group discussion might lead to a domestic disturbance requiring intervention from the local authorities. Try to avoid this.

From Two to Three Dimensions

Once you've collected everyone's ideas, it's time to make use of that graph paper—as long as you heed a couple of important warnings.

The most creative people can be rendered robotic when faced with a sheet of graph paper. Just because there are little blue squares all over the page in a perfect grid pattern doesn't mean you aren't allowed to draw a curve, or draw a line *in-between* two of the printed lines. Remember, *you* are the one determining the plans, not the graph paper.

While virtually every book ever written on the subject of home landscaping stresses the importance of committing a plan to paper, the abstract, precise nature of the process presents some hazards. Yes, it's important to know the dimensions of the lot, which direction the prevailing winds blow, what the exposure of the yard is (morning or afternoon sun or shade), the location of water spigots, electrical outlets, etc., etc. But there's something seductive in putting these hard-and-fast facts down on paper that makes it possible to lose sight of the personal spirit of the project.

If you think you may be subject to the tyranny of graph paper, neutralize its effect by starting the composition of the plan outdoors. To do this, take your backyard scrapbook to the backyard, along with a few dozen 12-inch wooden stakes, a half-dozen 2" x 2" x 6' wooden stakes (available at any lumberyard), a spool of heavy cotton string (500 feet should do), a couple of long garden hoses, two handfuls of clothespins, and a few old bed sheets. An odd list of equipment, to be sure, but it works.

Put your equipment aside for a moment and take a good look at your scrapbook. What have you got? You may have some ideas for fences, a play area for the kids, a deck or patio, perhaps a gazebo or arbor, a really great treehouse, an outside eating and cooking area, a lawn laid out with games in mind, or even a fountain, swimming pool, or spa. Your challenge

YOUR BACKYARD SCRAPBOOK MAY TAKE ON A LIFE OF ITS OWN, CONTINUING LONG AFTER THE DESIGN, CONSTRUCTION, AND PLANTING PROCESS IS COMPLETE. IF YOU INCLUDE A FEW BEFORE AND AFTER PHOTOGRAPHS, NOTES ON PLANTS THAT MAY OR MAY NOT HAVE GROWN WELL FOR YOU, RECEIPTS FOR MAJOR PURCHASES, WARRANTIES AND INSTRUCTIONS FOR MECHANICAL THINGS (SUCH AS THE SUBMERSIBLE PUMP YOU BOUGHT FOR YOUR POND OR A SET OF OUTDOOR LIGHTS), YOUR BACKYARD SCRAPBOOK WILL BECOME AN IMPORTANT RESOURCE. OVER A PERIOD OF YEARS, IT MAY EVEN TAKE ON THE STATUS OF A "DOCUMENT," CHRONICLING THE DEVELOPMENT OF A UNIQUE CREATIVE PROJECT.

"You should have heard me howl at some of those family meetings. Didn't make a darn bit of difference."

23

is to arrange the elements you want in the space available. To successfully meet this challenge, you should intimately know every corner of your backyard. You may *think* you know it, but you'd be surprised at how many people are locked into only one viewing position, usually about six feet away from the back door.

The Backyard Walkabout

Get acquainted with your yard by walking its perimeter, and I do mean the perimeter—no further than an arm's length from the lot line, please. While you walk, keep looking back at your house. Is there a spot, somewhere towards the rear or to the side of the yard where the view of your house is particularly pleasant? Would this be the best place for a small patio, just right for a couple of chairs and a couple of cool ones as evening shadows fall? Or is there a spot beneath a group of mature trees at the back of the yard that you discover to be delightfully shady? Conventional wisdom has it that outdoor eating areas should be located as close to the house as possible, but a big picnic table under that far-off leafy canopy just might be the nicest place to enjoy a meal.

And is that the perfect, almost horizontal limb on which to hang a swing? How about the area behind the shrubbery and under the tree, in the far corner of your lot…did you feel a sense of security and diminished scale that reminds you of places you liked to play in as a child? Perhaps this is the spot for a little "secret garden" for the kids in your house. All that's necessary is a layer of fine bark, perhaps a couple of sawed-off logs to use as table and chairs, and a playful adult to lead the way.

Your backyard "walkabout" may result in some new ideas about where some of the elements you want should go. This is the easiest (not to mention least expensive) time to change your mind—repeatedly, if desired. And even though they may not be in your immediate future, it's important to take into consideration *all* the elements of your "dream" backyard. This is the only way to make sure there's room for everything, that the various elements come together in a harmonious way, and that you don't build a concrete patio where you might eventually want to dig a hole for a small pond.

HOW ABOUT THE AREA BEHIND THE SHRUBBERY AND UNDER THE TREE, IN THE FAR CORNER OF YOUR LOT…DID YOU FEEL A SENSE OF SECURITY AND DIMINISHED SCALE THAT REMINDED YOU OF PLACES YOU LIKED TO PLAY IN AS A CHILD? PERHAPS THIS IS THE SPOT FOR A LITTLE "SECRET GARDEN" FOR THE KIDS IN YOUR HOUSE.

The next step is to mock the various elements into position, using the stakes, string, and sheets. Any rectilinear feature, such as a deck, patio, swimming pool, or sandbox can be outlined using the stakes and string. Simply pound the stakes a few inches into the ground and tie the string around the stakes to show the outline. Curved areas, such as lawns and planting beds are easily outlined using a long garden hose. Adjust the curves in the hose until the shape is pleasing from all angles. *Note:* Before deciding how large to make your lawn, please read "A Case for Lawns" on page 47.

To the person with little or no involvement in your design process, this mocked-up backyard will appear a motley mess. Where someone else sees only a sheet hanging from a line, you see a brick and latticework fence. That garden hose, lying in a curve on the dirt, isn't just lying there; it's marking the boundaries of a lush green lawn. And with the help of a little imagination, those four stakes over there in the shade of the tree are transformed into a sandbox where a child contentedly plays. The best part of this exercise is the three-dimensional quality it gives your emerging plan, something almost impossible to achieve with only pencil and paper, which happens to be the next step.

Committing the Plan to Paper, Finally

Leave the stakes, strings, sheets, and hoses in place for a couple of days or weeks if necessary. See how the arrangement looks at different times of the day and in different weather conditions. Once you're comfortable with the layout, get out the tape measure, pencils, and paper.

Make a rough drawing of the shape of your lot and house. (Please note the term "rough." Even those who feel that they simply can't draw anything should go ahead and "rough in" a drawing; it has to make sense to only one person—you—at this point.) Use this rough plan to note the actual measurements. Start by measuring the outside perimeter of your lot. Next, measure in from the lot lines to the outside walls of your house to establish its position on the lot. After this, start measuring the outlines of your deck, patio, play area, pool, and sandbox. To correctly position everything on the plan, you'll need to measure in from the lot line, just as you did with your house. And, yes, now is the

"Who needs a backyard walkabout? I already know every inch of this place like the back of my paw."

time to indicate the location of the water spigots, electrical outlets, and whatever else you think should be taken into consideration.

Once you have the measurements on the rough plan, transfer them to the graph paper and make a nice, tidy drawing—one that you can show with pride to any landscaper, architect, or building contractor. (Or, if you are concerned about your inability to draw, have someone who *can* draw do it for you, with you sitting there explaining what all of those strange lines and squiggles mean.) If a single sheet of graph paper is too confining, tape several sheets together to make a bigger drawing.

By the time you have the finished plan on paper, you should be confident that it reflects reality, rather than an abstract, two-dimensional drawing pulled together at the kitchen table. This, combined with your backyard scrapbook, will hold you in good stead as you go about making your plan come to life.

Making It Real

Now's the time for you to face another kind of reality—the fiscal kind. Putting cost estimates together can be a very time-consuming job, and it may be something you'd rather leave to a professional. This, of course, depends on whether you intend to do the work yourself or hire someone else to do it for you. Although this is largely a personal decision, it should be pointed out that most backyard construction (with the exception of pools, spas, fountains, and sophisticated electrical work) is well within the ability of a person with average mechanical ability. If you enjoy these kinds of projects, by all means have at it. You'll save considerable labor charges and experience a great deal of pride once the project is completed.

If, however, you decide you have neither the time nor the inclination to do the work yourself, a variety of professionals and semi-professionals are available. The type of help you choose depends both on the complexity of your plans and any personal contacts you have in the field. You may be better off using someone with whom you have a relationship that goes beyond a mere contract. The vagaries of contracting any type of work to a person unknown to you are well-documented. An already established personal relationship with any contractor could be your best insurance for the successful completion of the project.

You have many choices for outside help. They are presented here in traditional order of "professionalism" (that is, from the least to most amount of training and licensing required to use the title): nursery or garden center design/construction service, landscape designer, landscape contractor, landscape architect. On the straight construction side, there are carpenters, building designers, construction contractors, and architects. Some of these titles may differ from one part of the country to the other, but, regardless of the title, you'll be able to find someone at each level of skill no matter where you live.

Some people claim that you're always better off using only the top professionals in the field. This is certainly true with large and complex projects. But if your project is of small or moderate size, it's possible to get excellent results from general handypeople, retirees with extra time on their hands, and all manner of artists and craftspeople who are looking to augment their income.

Be forewarned that this will not be the type of working relationship where you can go away for a two-week vacation and expect the project to be finished upon your return. Any time construction is in progress, someone will need to be on hand to answer questions, respond to suggested changes in the plan, and to make sure that the work is proceeding in, shall we say, a timely manner.

Lay in a good supply of cold beverages and be prepared to put up with a sometimes erratic work schedule, as well as the possibility of interesting discourses on a variety of topics, from society and politics to interpersonal relationships. But if you know what you want, this type of outside help can work out very well.

Once the construction of your backyard actually begins, an odd thing happens. As soon as the first section of fence is hammered into place, or the outline of your future lawn is marked on the ground, your imagination takes over and completes the project in your mind's eye. That's why ground-breaking ceremonies attract so much attention. A project that may have been discussed conceptually for years has finally begun the first step to reality. It may not be a 40-story skyscraper you're erecting, but as the creator of your own backyard, you'll experience plenty of excitement as you take the first concrete steps beyond those vaporous ideas and paper plans. Here's to your own private ground-breaking ceremony!

Outside Help

When you start looking for some help in either the design or construction of your backyard, the first place you might look is in the yellow pages of your telephone book. You may not think of your backyard as a landscape, but that's probably where you'll find the kind of help you're looking for—under the heading of "Landscape." Listings include landscape architects, landscape contractors, and landscape designers.

Although it's difficult to gauge the merits of one individual or firm from another based on the information in a telephone book, it's a good place to start. Just don't expect to find the service you need with the first call. Treat it as an interviewing process.

If the landscape service expresses an interest in your project (after you've described the type of help you need, the approximate size of your yard, and the size of your budget), it's time for you to ask some questions: How long have they been in business, do they specialize in a certain type of work, what type of contract do they offer, and is it possible to see some examples of their work and talk with previous clients? Be sure to take notes, and keep them in a file (or your backyard scrapbook) for future reference.

If the firm or individual you talk with determines that their talents are not suited to your needs, be sure to ask them for other recommendations. And once you find someone who fits the bill, don't stop there. It's surprising how much you can learn about the field simply by talking with a half-dozen or so people.

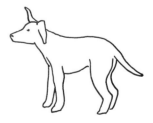

"'Bark at strangers. Don't bark.' I'm supposed to tell the difference between a contractor and a stranger?"

Requiring only a modest ability and relatively crude materials, most backyard building projects also go up quickly. The simple gate at right is embellished by the small cast-plaque shown in the above drawing. Sculptor George Carruth calls it "The Garden Smile."

BACKYARD BUILDING

Design and construction professionals call the non-living components of any landscape the "hardscape." It may not be the most appealing of words, but it aptly defines the nature of walls, fences, patios, decks, terraces, arbors, and walkways. If your goal is to create an outdoor living space, it is important to resist the temptation to plant the trees, shrubs, flowers, and vines you want until after the hardscape is in place. Both you and the plants will benefit from your patience.

When you walk through a pleasing yard, or look at a picture of one, your first impression will probably be of the plantings—the trees, shrubs, flowers, and vines. It is only on closer inspection that you realize how important the hardscape is in creating a pleasurable outdoor scene. The great English garden writer of the 19th century, Gertrude Jekyll, was very specific in her instructions for the creation of a garden: First and foremost, she said, it must have "good bones."

For the all-important "good bones" Miss Jekyll so admired, she turned to her partner, Edwin Lutyens. Sir Edwin (he was eventually to be knighted for his superlative design work) was a master of what we now term hardscape—walls, walkways, arbors, terraces, and the like. He had a great appreciation for the materials themselves, and used them in a style that respected the architectural traditions of the region, as well as the house the garden surrounded. This process was made easier by the fact that Sir Edwin often designed the house, as well.

Homeowners from one corner of America to the other

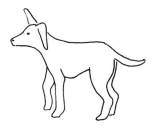

"I could tell that Miss Jekyll person a thing or two about 'good bones.'"

FENCES

FOR YEARS, THE "DOG-EARED" FENCE WAS THE STANDARD-ISSUE STYLE IN AMERICA. FORTUNATELY, THERE ARE MANY MORE OPTIONS TODAY.

PICKETS ARE READILY AVAILABLE IN A VARIETY OF STYLES, SUCH AS THIS GOTHIC VERSION. EACH HAS ITS OWN CHARM, APPROPRI-ATE TO A WIDE RANGE OF OLD-FASHIONED HOUSES.

THE JAPANESE ARE MASTERS OF GARDEN CONSTRUCTION, OFTEN CREATING FENCES THAT ARE AS DETAILED AS FURNITURE. THE PEAKED CAP IS A COMMON FEATURE.

ORNAMENTAL POSTS AND POST FINIALS MAKE FOR A "FINISHED" LOOK ON ALMOST ANY FENCE. AVAILABLE AT WELL-STOCKED BUILDING SUPPLY STORES.

ONE OF THE MOST PLEASING AND VERSATILE FENCE DESIGNS INCORPO-RATES A PANEL OF LATTICE AT THE TOP. GOOD FOR SUPPORTING VINES, TOO.

are beginning have a similar respect for the many and diverse architectural traditions this country has produced: the prairie houses of the Midwest, the colonial and various revival styles of New England, the derivative period houses of the South, the adobe and pueblo styles of the Southwest, and the craftsman, ranch, and Mediterranean houses of the West—to name just a few.

The best thing we can learn from Lutyens and Jekyll is that the architectural style of the hardscape should be an extension of the house itself or in harmony with its geographic location—unless, of course, one intends something to be intentionally whimsical or out-of-place. By respecting a particular architectural tradition or, in some rare occasions, by deliberately choosing not to, you will create a backyard of timeless character and appeal.

Fences

At the height of the natural landscape movement in the mid- to late-18th century, it was almost impossible to tell the difference between a fashionable garden and the surrounding native countryside, so seamlessly were the two woven together. Arbiters of taste, whose gardens were frequently measured in square miles rather than square feet, considered it a sign of an unenlightened, medieval mentality to even think about enclosing a garden in any way.

American attitudes regarding home landscapes developed during this period, when natural movements were popular, and a few of these biases continue to haunt us today. There are still a number of neighborhoods (indeed, whole geographic regions) where fences between houses are forbidden either by covenant or by custom. This is unfortunate because gardens are *meant* to be private places, whether the privacy was achieved by owning all of the land to the horizon or, for the rest of us, by enclosing our small plot in some way.

Even in areas where fences, walls, or hedges are permitted, there is the lingering fear by many that a fence or wall will somehow offend the neighbors on the other side or perhaps make those same neighbors suspicious of what's happening on your side. If your neighbors suspect that you're out in your backyard, barefoot and in your bathrobe, soaking up the morning sunshine and lingering over that first cup of coffee, I hope they're right. Unless you feel protected, you won't feel comfortable. And if you don't feel comfortable in your backyard, you'll probably spend very little time there.

Owners of lots larger than one-third acre in size may not fear the invasions from neighbor's inquiring eyes, dogs, noise, or traffic that the owner of a smaller lot does. Generally speaking, the smaller the yard and the closer the neighbors, the greater the need for some kind of privacy.

If covenants prevent you from constructing any kind of barrier, you may succeed in providing the desired privacy simply by planting a group of shrubs and evergreen trees (which branch all the way to the ground) in a strategic spot near the perimeter of the lot. This won't do anything about your neighbor's wandering pets and children, but it will allow you the luxury of taking a backyard morning stroll in that old bathrobe, or your pajamas, for that matter.

Fences, as opposed to walls or hedges, are the fastest and least expensive way to ensure privacy in a backyard. If, however, you have the funds and desire to build a stone, masonry, or brick wall, by all means do so. They are picturesque and appropriate to houses of almost any architectural style. Or, if you don't mind waiting the several years it takes for a hedge to grow tall and thick enough to provide privacy, go right ahead and plant one. Hedges, too, are complementary to virtually any architectural style, and there's nothing quite as pretty in an outdoor setting as a living wall of even, clipped green.

To ensure the results you want from any barrier, take a couple of 8-foot-long stakes, a long length of clothesline or strong twine, a handful of clothespins, and a couple of old sheets or blankets. Pound the stakes into the ground at either end of the line separating the yards, and tie the clothesline to the stakes at the height you think you want. Next, clip the sheets to the line with the clothespins and then step back to the part of the garden where you want the greatest privacy. If you can't see your neighbors (who, by now, certainly will have come out to see what's going on), you know how tall to make your fence.

Now that your neighbors are out there, ask them how they would feel about a fence between your properties. If they agree that a fence would be mutually beneficial, it is customary for both parties to share the cost of the fence. If so, the fence should be built directly on the property line. If

HANGING SHEETS FOR A MAKE-BELIEVE FENCE IS ALMOST CERTAIN TO LURE YOUR NEIGHBORS OUTDOORS. ONCE THEY'RE THERE, ASK THEM HOW THEY WOULD FEEL ABOUT A FENCE BETWEEN YOUR PROPERTIES.

"They'll probably be so relieved that you're not making a clothesline, they won't even care about the fence."

GATES

A SOLID WOODEN GATE, PAINTED IN A VIVID HUE, IS A SUITABLE CHOICE FOR MEDITERRA- NEAN, SPANISH, OR ADOBE ARCHITEC- TURE. THIS IS ESPECIALLY TRUE WHEN THE GATE IS CONTAINED IN A WHITE-WASHED PLASTER WALL.

LATTICE GATES AND FENCES REPRESENT A CLEAN, TIMELESS LOOK, APPROPRIATE TO ANY NUMBER OF ARCHITECTURE STYLES. TRADITIONALLY PAINTED WHITE, LATTICE ALSO LOOKS ATTRACTIVE IN VERY DARK SHADES OF GREEN, BROWN, OR EVEN BLACK.

THE ORNATE FORMALITY OF VICTORIAN ARCHITEC- TURE SPILLED OVER TO THE GARDEN. FENCES AND GATES WERE FREQUENTLY FASHIONED FROM WROUGHT-IRON MATERIAL, EASILY MANIPULATED INTO INTRICATE DESIGNS.

A SIMPLE BOARD AND RAIL FENCE AND GATE, WITH SPACES LEFT IN-BETWEEN, MAY NOT PROVIDE ULTIMATE PRIVACY, BUT THEY HAVE THEIR OWN CHARM AND DIGNITY. THEY ARE ESPECIALLY NICE WHEN THE PEEK-A-BOO VIEW BETWEEN THE BOARDS IS AN ENTICING ONE.

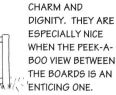

you want a fence and your neighbor doesn't, you'll have to forge ahead on your own as diplomatically as possible, paying for it yourself and locating it clearly on your side of the property line.

There was a time when the only commonly available fence style was the familiar "dog-eared" design. Fencing contractors and do-it-yourself outlets now offer any number of pleasing options, some of which are illustrated on page 30. As you make your decision about what type of fence to build, remember that a fence is a significant and long-lasting feature. It pays to go the extra "mile" and build a fence that is both visually and architecturally appealing.

Gates

The most simple definition of a gate, "an opening in a fence or wall," belies its symbolic importance. Ever since walls and fences have been built, the construction of gates and gateways has received special attention. The wall or fence itself was important, but it was the gate that announced to the world who or what was being kept out and who might be let in.

From the time you begin thinking about a gate, take into consideration the architecture of your house, the style of the adjoining fence, wall or hedge, how the gate fits in with the neighborhood or area it looks out on, and finally, whether or not it suits your taste.

A gate at the front of the property, the one that leads from the public street to private space around your house, should be given the most importance, both in size and design detail. Other gates, such as those leading to the backyard or through a side yard, or a gate contained within the yard itself, are traditionally of less stature. Generally speaking, if your house is of a particular style, be it Mediterranean, colonial, Victorian, or ranch, the design of the fence, wall, and gate should follow suit.

Gates can be divided between those you can see through and those you can't. Although it's a fine point, see-through gates, such as wrought iron or an open wood design, are best used when the background (what you see behind the gate) is simple and uncluttered, such as lawn, a clipped evergreen hedge, or even a wall. In these situations, the detail of the gate can be appreciated instead of being lost to a complex pattern of vegetation.

If you choose a solid gate, think about adding a peep-hole. It serves a utilitarian function, allowing you to see what's on the other side of the gate, much like the small windows in the swinging doors found in restaurant kitchens. Aesthetically, peep-holes add a bit of interest to even the simplest of gates. Open-fretwork Oriental tiles, ornamental wrought iron, or even a small square of lattice will nicely cover a peep-hole. Or take a look in architectural renovation catalogs and select one of my favorites: ornamental metal heat register covers. The Victorian designs are intricate in detail and well-suited to a garden setting, much more so than in their intended location, on the floor of your house.

While you are still in the planning stages, think about whether or not you want to light the gate, have an intercom or doorbell installed, or have access to a security system. All of these require electricity, which is far easier to include *during* construction. If you want to be able to lock your gate, purchase the locking mechanism first so the gate can be built to the lock's mechanical specifications.

A typical gate receives heavy use. Repeated opening and closing (not to mention the occasional slamming), exposure to weather, and the inevitable swinging upon by youngsters will all take their toll. It's best to plan on these abuses from the beginning, rather than try to change both human and mother nature. The posts that hold up the gate are a good place to start.

How far apart the posts or pillars will be is a deceptively simple but important consideration, especially if you will ever be passing through them with a loaded wheelbarrow, perambulator or other wide load. The minimum practical opening is 36 inches; the wider the opening, of course, the wider the gate will be. Depending on what it is made of, a gate more than 48 inches wide should be in two parts, opening in the middle.

If you are using wooden posts, 4 x 4s will do, but 6 x 6s are better. They should be buried in concrete, 30 to 36 inches in the ground. Power posthole diggers, which make quick work of digging postholes, can be rented by the hour from rental yards, and premixed concrete is available in manageable-sized sacks from your building supply store. Use a level to make sure the posts are standing up straight,

IF YOU CHOOSE A SOLID GATE, THINK ABOUT ADDING A PEEP-HOLE. IT SERVES A UTILITARIAN FUNCTION, ALLOWING YOU TO SEE WHAT'S ON THE OTHER SIDE OF THE GATE, MUCH LIKE THE SMALL WINDOWS IN THE SWINGING DOORS FOUND IN RESTAURANT KITCHENS.

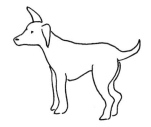

"I may not be able to see through the peep-hole, but I can see your feet. Now let me in, darn it."

33

DECKS

BACKYARD OWNERS BEWARE: AS CONVENIENT AS THEY MAY BE, THE DECK "KITS" OFFERED BY SOME LUMBER STORES MAY WIND UP LOOKING LIKE THE PROVERBIAL WART ON A HOG. AS LONG-LIVED AND USEFUL AS DECKS ARE, YOU MIGHT AS WELL GO TO THE EXTRA EFFORT AND CONSTRUCT A MORE DISTINC-TIVE ADDITION.

SIMPLE DETAILS, SUCH AS A NOTCH CUT OUT OF EACH FACING BOARD ON THE RAILING, CAN ADD A GRACE NOTE TO AN OTHERWISE PLAIN DECK.

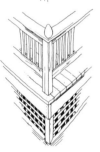

OLDER HOMES BENEFIT FROM A DECK WITH A FEW DESIGN DETAILS, ESPECIALLY IN THE RAILINGS, POSTS, AND SURROUNDING APRON.

FREESTANDING DECKS CAN BE BUILT ANYWHERE THEY'RE NEEDED—FOR SUNBATHING, OUTDOOR DINING, OR CONTEMPLAT-ING A BEAUTIFUL VIEW. AS CLOSE AS THEY ARE TO THE GROUND, MOST CAN BE CONSTRUCTED WITHOUT RAILS.

then secure them with temporary braces until the concrete sets up; give it 24 hours.

Brick posts should also be set in a concrete foundation, and hangers for the gate hinges should be embedded in the brick as the pillars are built, rather than added as an after-thought. Because of these special considerations, it may be a good idea to have brick pillars professionally constructed.

Decks and Other Stable Surfaces

When it comes to building decks, form and location follow function. A deck primarily intended for sunbathing obviously needs to be located where there's plenty of sun and a modicum of privacy, requirements that may demand it be a free-standing unit, not attached to the house. A deck for rustic outdoor dining might be ideally located in a stand of trees at the far corner of your lot, again completely separate from the house. The most simple free-standing deck, what some would call a wooden platform rather than a deck, looks perfectly at home in a wide variety of backyard settings.

Most people, however, prefer a deck attached directly to the house. In their favor, decks constructed right next to a house effectively and effortlessly extend indoor living space into the great outdoors, making the pleasures of your back-yard even more immediately accessible and inviting. In these situations, however, decks can also be at their worst. The truth is that decks don't belong on every house—unless you're willing to go to some extra effort in the design and detail department.

That said, on what kind of houses do decks naturally belong? Before answering that question, it helps to know where the concept of outdoor decks originated. With their reverence for nature and love of natural beauty, Japanese designers and builders have for centuries sought ways to bring the inhabitants of houses in closer proximity with the natural world. Wide, uncovered porches were built around Japanese houses to take maximum advantage of pleasing views, be it a rising moon, a lake, fall foliage or a blossoming cherry tree. Today's decks are directly related to the uncov-ered porches attached to both grand and humble Japanese homes.

During the 1950s and '60s, certain types of modern residential architecture developed in this country that highlighted indoor/outdoor living. While the styles may have differed, postwar housing design was similar in spirit to traditional Japanese architecture. Both placed importance on versatile, open interior space, and both stressed a more intimate relationship between the house and its natural surroundings. Patios and decks were natural accompaniments to these houses.

Time has not diluted the popularity of decks and the casual lifestyle they represent. Over the past 30 or 40 years, however, certain styles and design details, including railings, benches and stairs, have become inextricably linked with the general notion of a deck. But remember, what may be appropriate for the deck may not be appropriate for the house to which the deck is attached.

Which brings us back to the question, where does the common wood deck rightfully belong?

Unpainted wood decks, left to weather naturally, are perfectly at home attached to ranch and craftsman style houses, mountain and lakeside cabins, and houses built in the Japanese style. Once you move into any other style house—be it Cape Cod, colonial, Mediterranean, Tudor, Victorian, or Georgian—an unfinished wood deck appears out of character.

Look carefully at the exterior of your house, taking note of any architectural detail on railings, balusters, windows, and roof lines. Can those details be re-created in the deck railings, stairs, or hand rails? Can the "apron" that surrounds the deck be finished in a similar or complementary style?

If it's impossible to match the base of the deck with the foundation of the house, "ground" the deck by enclosing the bottom sides in some fashion. Lattice panels are ideal for this purpose and will complement almost any architectural style.

In addition to keeping the architectural style in mind, there's one more important thing you can do to blend a new deck with your house: Paint it. This suggestion brings howls of protest from those who admire lumber's natural weathered look and from those who fear that painting anything outdoors will require constant upkeep. But a new generation of stains has been created that are specially formulated for outdoor use. They are so opaque, they look like paint rather than a stain, a fact that will further help visually tie the

AS FUNCTIONAL AS DECKS ARE, THERE ARE ALSO TIMES WHEN IT'S GOOD TO SPREAD A BLANKET ON THE LAWN FOR A PICNIC, OR TO HANG A HAMMOCK UNDER THE PINES.

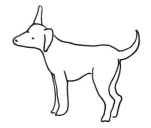

"The best thing about that deck is all the scraps left behind under the picnic table."

OVERHEADS

IN AREAS OF HARSH, HOT SUN OR FREQUENT RAINS, A SOLID WOOD OVERHEAD MAY BE JUST THE THING FOR PLEASANT OUTDOOR LIVING. IN MOST CASES, IT'S BEST TO MATCH THE OVERHEAD TO THE EXISTING ROOF OF THE HOUSE, CONSTRUCTING IT OF THE SAME MATERIAL AND STYLE.

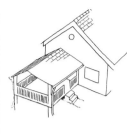

A LATTICE OVERHEAD IS ONE OF THE MOST PLEASANT OF ALL CHOICES. ITS OPEN CONSTRUCTION ALLOWS FREE AIR CIRCULATION, MODIFIES THE EFFECTS OF THE SUN, AND CREATES A LOVELY LIGHT-AND-SHADE PATTERN.

OLD-FASHIONED AWNINGS ARE APPROPRIATE TO ALMOST ANY ARCHITECTURAL STYLE AND REALLY "DRESS-UP" THE APPEARANCE OF YOUR HOUSE.

HOW ABOUT A FREE-STANDING OVERHEAD TO COVER THAT SPECIAL GARDEN BENCH? WITH A FEW VINES ENTWINED, IT COULD CREATE THE HEIGHT OF CHARM.

THE SIMPLEST OF ALL AWNINGS ARE ALSO AMONG THE MOST SOPHISTICATED. WITHOUT SIDES, AND HELD UP WITH ORNAMENTAL POLES, THESE AWNINGS MAKE A DISTINCTIVE ADDITION TO ANY OUTDOOR SETTING.

deck with your house. Ask at your local paint or supply store for recommendations; these new stains are available from a variety of manufacturers in a wide range of colors. In most cases, stains, which penetrate the wood, will actually help preserve the deck and require a minimum of upkeep (unlike regular paint). By staining the floor of the deck to match the color of the outside walls of your house, and the railings to match the color of the trim, you will go a long way in achieving a harmonious picture. So much so, in fact, that you could begin to view your deck as simply another room of your house. But beware. Its comfort and convenience may lead you to forget about the rest of the backyard.

As functional as decks are, there are also times when it's good to spread a blanket on the lawn for a picnic, or to hang a hammock under the pines. Out on the lawn, you'll see your yard—and your deck—from an entirely different perspective. You may even find that you've been overlooking some of the finer pleasures your yard has to offer.

Other Stable Surfaces

Aside from decks, traditional outdoor flooring includes concrete, flagstone, brick, and, occasionally, asphalt. Poured concrete slabs are widely used for patios. In its favor, concrete is relatively inexpensive, quick to install, and permanent. Detractors say concrete is "too hard" to be at home in an intimate outdoor setting and dislike the glare it produces. Both objections can be circumvented with an "exposed aggregate" finish, which results in a more natural-looking, pebbly surface, and no glare.

Flagstone and brick fit right into almost any outdoor situation, bringing warmth and character to the scene. And, yes, both are time-consuming and expensive to install. In most cases, a layer of sand is needed under the bricks or stones. In very cold or damp locations, additional precautions may be necessary. When you choose either brick or flagstone, you are choosing to make an investment in your backyard; only you can determine whether or not it will be a worthy expenditure.

Asphalt, that utilitarian outdoor surface, is also the least suitable for most residential uses. As well as it holds up on roads, sharp objects—such as table and chair legs and high-heeled shoes—take their toll on this relatively soft surface. It is, however, a good surface for driveways and service areas.

Overhead Protection

The most beautiful overhead protection in any backyard setting is the dense, leafy canopy provided by a mature shade tree. Unfortunately, the place where you'd really like to sit in the shade may not be graced by such a tree or, conversely, the place where the tree is growing may not be where you want the protection. These are situations when, if you want *immediate* protection, it must be constructed, rather than grown.

Outdoor overhead protection is used as a shield against the sun or rain, or to keep from being directly in your neighbor's line of sight, especially from second-story windows. If you don't mind the rain, there are many construction options, with lattice and lath being perennial favorites. Depending on how much sun you want to allow through, the lathwork can be constructed in a tight or loose design. Either way, the resulting shade pattern below will create a dappled effect, pleasant for both plants and people.

If you need total protection from the elements, what you build overhead will be more like the roof on your house. In fact, simply copying whatever your roof is made from, whether it's cedar shakes or composition shingles, is one of the best ways to visually tie the outdoor structure to the house. Or consider having an awning made. In addition to standard canvas or vinylized material (which offer protection from rain), many new awning products are available, including some that allow sunlight and air to filter through.

Both options, latticework and awnings, are classics. They have been used for generations in a wide variety of settings, to the point where either looks right at home with almost any architectural style. The only material to avoid, one quite popular a few years back, is corrugated fiberglass. Although it is easy to use, corrugated fiberglass is difficult to harmoniously incorporate into an outdoor situation.

Arbors and Pergolas

Some overhead structures are intended not for protection but as support for vining plants. Arbors and pergolas fall into this category. Although they are sometimes confused, a pergola is a free-standing, open-roofed structure (with a few

THE MOST BEAUTIFUL OVERHEAD PROTECTION IN ANY BACKYARD SETTING IS THE DENSE, LEAFY CANOPY PROVIDED BY A MATURE SHADE TREE.

"Second-best thing about a tree: its shade."

37

GAZEBOS

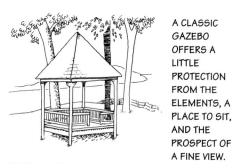

A CLASSIC GAZEBO OFFERS A LITTLE PROTECTION FROM THE ELEMENTS, A PLACE TO SIT, AND THE PROSPECT OF A FINE VIEW. IF THEY SEEM TO REPRESENT A LEISURELY, GENTEEL WAY OF LIFE, REMINISCENT OF AN EARLIER TIME, YOU'LL KNOW THAT THE DESIGN OF YOUR GAZEBO HAS SUCCEEDED.

GAZEBOS, AS WHIMSICAL AS THEY ARE, OFTEN RECEIVE CONSIDERABLE ATTENTION TO DETAIL. THE PREVAILING FEELING SEEMS TO BE, IF IT'S GOING TO BE SEEN AS A FOLLY, YOU MIGHT AS WELL MAKE IT A FULL-FLEDGED ONE! A CASE IN POINT: THIS GOTHIC-STYLE GAZEBO.

LITTLE MORE THAN A PERMANENT UMBRELLA, THIS THATCHED, SIDELESS SHADE STRUCTURE WOULD BE RIGHT AT HOME IN A RUSTIC SETTING WHERE A MORE FORMAL GAZEBO MIGHT APPEAR OUT OF CHARACTER.

connecting pieces of lumber for the vines to attach themselves to), while an arbor is most often constructed over a walkway connecting one building or living area to another. The key to success with either an arbor or a pergola is to build them to last. Use the heaviest lumber consistent with the scale of your yard, use long screws to hold the timbers together instead of nails, and if you plan on painting it, do it right the first time: It's practically impossible to repaint an arbor or pergola once it's covered with a vine; most vining plants, such as wisteria, grapevines, honeysuckle, trumpetvine, and the like, are rampant growers.

Gazebos

Like the caterpillar that changes into a butterfly, the gazebo started out as a belvedere. And what, you may ask, is a belvedere? Back when castles and moats were all the rage, belvederes were small, solid-roofed structures, built right into a fortress wall for use as look-out posts. Over time, the belvedere came down from the fortress wall and planted itself in the garden, but retained its "look-out" character. Today, it would be difficult to find someone to argue the fine points of distinction between a gazebo and a belvedere, so call it what you will. A gazebo or belvedere is a distinctive addition to any backyard, still at its best if located where it affords a view and a little protection from the elements, if not the advancing enemy.

Hardly a necessity, you may have your heart set on a gazebo, nonetheless. It doesn't have to be built tomorrow, or even a year from now. Dream about it for a while.

Closely associated in this country with the Victorian era, many of today's gazebos have retained their gingerbread character. Considering, however, that gazebos are by their very nature fanciful, there's no reason to stick with a particular architectural style or even to tie the architecture of the gazebo to that of your house. Gazebos and fantasy are natural partners. If you've always wanted a gazebo that looked like a Japanese tea house even though you live in a two-story Tudor, there's nothing to stop you from making that fantasy a reality.

An often overlooked function for a gazebo is as a protected spot for outdoor dining. Because most gazebos are constructed with seating around the interior perimeter, all that's needed is a table. Any meal becomes a memorable event when taken in the gazebo, and it's perfect for special occasions such as birthday parties (gazebos look great done up in balloons and streamers), or a late-night, make-up, just-the-two-of-you dinner, with lots of votive candles, small portions of extravagant food, some flowers from the garden…well, you get the picture.

Secret Retreats

Back in the time when gardens were designed on a grand scale, extravagant "eye-catchers" were frequently built at the far corner of a garden. An eye-catcher was a building that might look like the ruins of a classical building, a Chinese temple, or a miniature castle. That they were also called "follies" is telling: They were whimsical, surprising bits of architecture meant to add visual interest to the landscape. According to written descriptions from the times, these places were often used as the location for clandestine assignations and midnight rendezvous. Other, less intriguing uses included dinner parties, a place to read, study, or paint, or as a quiet place to simply contemplate the sweet mysteries of life.

While it may seem like a folly to even consider such a place for your own yard, a secret retreat doesn't have to be grand or architecturally significant. All such a place needs to provide is privacy. While it may sound somewhat impractical—eccentric, even—a hideaway of one type or another may become the favorite place in your backyard. If you're concerned about keeping visible manifestations of your eccentricities to a minimum, secret retreats can be constructed under the guise of any number of practical purposes—a toolshed, a lath house, potting shed, or greenhouse, to name a few.

Disguises for Secret Retreats

To have a personal private place within your backyard is like having a treat within a delight. As a child, I was fortunate to experience four such secret retreats. The first two, a screened-in, tree-shaded sandbox and a tiny under-the-stairs greenhouse, were in my grandparents' garden. The other two, a tree house in a huge pear tree and a small private garden I designed on my own, were part of my parents' backyard.

IF YOU'RE CONCERNED ABOUT KEEPING VISIBLE MANIFESTATIONS OF YOUR ECCENTRICITIES TO A MINIMUM, SECRET RETREATS CAN BE CONSTRUCTED UNDER THE GUISE OF ANY NUMBER OF PRACTICAL PURPOSES—A TOOLSHED, LATH HOUSE, POTTING SHED, GREENHOUSE, OR JUST AN ANONYMOUS "OUTBUILDING."

"He goes in that little room to 'meditate'? Who's he kidding? I can hear the snoring from here."

39

TREE HOUSES & SECRET RETREATS

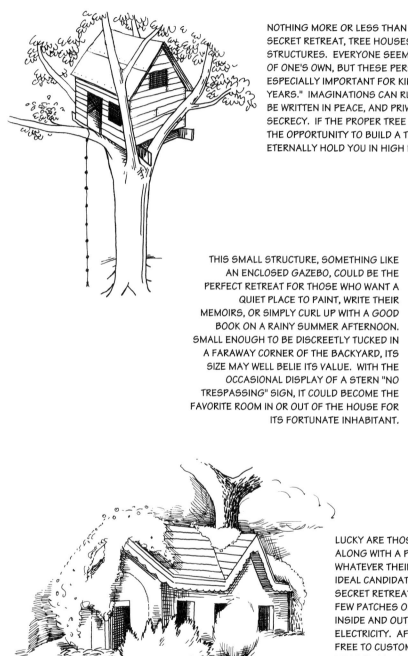

NOTHING MORE OR LESS THAN A CHILD'S VERSION OF A SECRET RETREAT, TREE HOUSES ARE INDEED SPECIAL STRUCTURES. EVERYONE SEEMS TO BENEFIT FROM A ROOM OF ONE'S OWN, BUT THESE PERSONAL PLACES ARE ESPECIALLY IMPORTANT FOR KIDS DURING THE "WONDER YEARS." IMAGINATIONS CAN RUN UNBRIDLED, DIARIES CAN BE WRITTEN IN PEACE, AND PRIVATE CLUBS ORGANIZED IN SECRECY. IF THE PROPER TREE IS AVAILABLE, DON'T WASTE THE OPPORTUNITY TO BUILD A TREE HOUSE. YOUR KIDS WILL ETERNALLY HOLD YOU IN HIGH REGARD FOR YOUR EFFORTS.

THIS SMALL STRUCTURE, SOMETHING LIKE AN ENCLOSED GAZEBO, COULD BE THE PERFECT RETREAT FOR THOSE WHO WANT A QUIET PLACE TO PAINT, WRITE THEIR MEMOIRS, OR SIMPLY CURL UP WITH A GOOD BOOK ON A RAINY SUMMER AFTERNOON. SMALL ENOUGH TO BE DISCREETLY TUCKED IN A FARAWAY CORNER OF THE BACKYARD, ITS SIZE MAY WELL BELIE ITS VALUE. WITH THE OCCASIONAL DISPLAY OF A STERN "NO TRESPASSING" SIGN, IT COULD BECOME THE FAVORITE ROOM IN OR OUT OF THE HOUSE FOR ITS FORTUNATE INHABITANT.

LUCKY ARE THOSE WHO INHERIT AN OLD OUTBUILDING ALONG WITH A PREVIOUSLY OWNED HOUSE. WHATEVER THEIR ORIGINAL PURPOSE, THEY ARE IDEAL CANDIDATES FOR TRANSFORMING INTO A SECRET RETREAT. ALL THAT MAY BE NEEDED ARE A FEW PATCHES ON THE ROOF, A QUICK PAINT JOB INSIDE AND OUT, AND THE POSSIBLE ADDITION OF ELECTRICITY. AFTER THAT, YOU'RE ON YOUR OWN, FREE TO CUSTOMIZE THE STRUCTURE TO YOUR HEART'S CONTENT. IF THERE'S SUCH AN OUT-BUILDING IN YOUR BACKYARD, DON'T OVERLOOK ITS POTENTIAL.

The screened-in sandbox was tucked away in the far corner of my grandmother's garden. The sides of the sandbox were constructed of 2x10's, with a very simple, box-like frame above it, covered with a fine-mesh metal screen, making the whole thing look a little like an aviary. At the time, I didn't realize the screen served the practical purpose of keeping the neighborhood cats from using the sandbox as a litterbox. All I knew was that to be let into that enclosed space by my grandmother, empty coffee cans and spoon measures in hand, was to enter a magical sandcastle world of my own.

The greenhouse, which was built under the back stairs of my grandparents' city house, was so small that you could barely turn around once you were inside. But as the doors were closed behind me, I was in an exotic, tropical world without boundaries, where it was easy to become lost for hours.

THE FOCAL POINT OF MY SECRET GARDEN WAS A JAPANESE CERAMIC FISH BOWL COMPLETE WITH GOLDFISH. THE FISH BOWL WAS STRATEGICALLY PLACED UNDER THE WEEPING ELM, RESTING ON ITS SOFT BED OF IRISH MOSS.

There couldn't have been more than a dozen potted plants on the bench—vining philodendrons, angel-wing begonias, geraniums and cuttings of treasured plants rooting in jars of water. No matter. The space was enclosed, moist and warm, exuding that pungent odor of rich soil and living things. Sunlight through the little panes created a leafy stained-glass window in a hundred shades of green. After repeated attempts at calling me, my grandmother would finally have to come down and knock on the window in an effort to pull me out of that world and upstairs to lunch.

Back home, my father built me a tree house deep within an ancient pear tree. Well, not exactly a tree house…it turned out be a platform high above the ground, without walls or a roof. Climbing up that wobbly ladder for the first time, to the safety of the platform, was quite an experience. Even better was the realization that once there, the rope ladder could be pulled up, making me impervious from ground invasions. Talk about a retreat!

Although it was used as a staging area for an occasional and fabulous rotten pear war with hapless friends on the ground below, more often that protected aerie was where I retreated to write in my journal, read, and disappear when the wild dogs of adolescence were hard upon my heels. For a number of years, I probably spent as much time in that tree house as I did in school—and may have learned as much there as in any classroom.

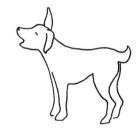

"It was nice of him to put that big bowl of water out, but what are those fish doing in there?"

41

I made my last childhood retreat myself by commandeering an out-of-the-way corner in my parents' backyard, about nine by twelve feet in size, and created a garden of my own. I built a small wooden deck in the middle of the space, with raised planting beds on either side and a square opening in the middle of the deck.

The small opening in the middle of the deck received special attention. Infatuated at the time with Japanese gardens, I filled this 30-inch square space with a small Japanese elm of a particularly artistic shape, some Irish moss, a couple of craggy rocks, and as the focal point, a Japanese ceramic fish bowl complete with goldfish. (I remember all of this very clearly because of the number of trips it took on my bicycle to procure these supplies.) The fish bowl was strategically placed under the weeping elm, resting on a soft bed of Irish moss.

One spring night, as I walked through that little garden, I noticed that the full moon was perfectly reflected in the surface of the water in the fish bowl. In addition to the moon, the reflection included an extraordinary mixture of pale pear blossoms from the neighboring tree and from far beyond, the twinkling stars. Sensing my presence, the goldfish rose to the surface, quickly rippling and distorting the picture.

Although gone in an instant, that brief moment of magic convinced me forevermore that even in the smallest of gardens it was indeed possible to combine heaven and earth. That such a moment occurred in my own secret garden made the experience even richer and more memorable.

A secret retreat is the perfect spot to display those "treasures" valuable only to their owner.

A Practical Disguise

At the turn of this century, practically all backyards had at least one "outbuilding," usually at the far end of the lot, tucked behind a few trees and bushes. Today these have been largely replaced by prefabricated metal sheds, notably lacking in charm and certainly the last place anyone might think of using as a hideaway.

Old-fashioned outbuildings were originally intended for practical uses, from tool storage to potting shed. But over time many of these simple sheds developed into something far more unique and personal. With each passing year, it wasn't unusual for the little building to take on more of the owner's personality and for the owner to spend more time in his miniature home away from home. Postcards and calendar pictures might be thumb-tacked to the unpainted walls. Perhaps a collection of smooth granite stones were placed on view in the windowsill. An odd assortment of artifacts, unearthed while digging in the garden, might be set upon one corner of the workbench. Pretty shards of porcelain or crockery, old medicine bottles the colors of jewels, and a couple of old handle-less hand tools were as artfully arranged as any museum display of archaeological treasures.

In many ways, these outbuildings became a grown-up version of that fort you may have had as a child—a place of refuge—a part of, yet apart from, that place called home. In an era when we seem to be perennially short on space, an extra spot out there in the backyard is just the thing to provide a little breathing room, the place you go to when you need to be alone.

When used for a hobby such as oil painting, pottery making, or model building, there's the added benefit of being able to leave your work in progress, along with all of its attendant tools and supplies, rather than having to gather everything up after you've finished with each day's work. Activities notorious for disturbing others, such as drum practice, voice lessons, or cigar smoking, can be carried out in harmless obscurity.

Building a shed is a straightforward proposition, demanding only the most rudimentary of carpentry skills, well within the range of the average do-it-yourselfer. If your skill level happens to fall below average, a carpenter will be able to build the structure in just a few days time if supplied with some simple drawings and dimensions. Before starting on such a project, check with your local building department to ensure that your project meets with their requirements.

The key is to keep the project modest. Your tool shed sanctuary can be constructed from second-hand lumber, windows and doors from the salvage yard, and the barest minimum of amenities. Electricity is probably a must, but running water, indoor plumbing, heat or air-conditioning, carpeting, rain gutters and downspouts, insulation, and paint for the walls all fall into the "optional" category. Don't fix up the place too much; the appeal of these small buildings is often in their rustic character.

Once it is constructed, take a few steps to incorporate your new home away from home into its setting. Pre-made lattice panels can be nailed to the exterior walls as support for vining plants. A small arbor over the door, covered with a climbing rose or other flowering vine, has a timeless appeal. And a wooden bench pulled up next to the shed may become a favorite sitting place for lunch or your morning coffee.

Whether you use it as a place to get away from it all, or as the spot that allows you the freedom to throw pots (or maybe pans, depending on your mood), build that replica of the *Hispaniola*, or do calligraphy, the most modest of sheds will pay rich returns: peace of mind, complete involvement with an activity that pleases you, and a place to contain it.

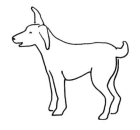

"The next time he gives me any trouble I'm going to lead the missus straight to where he hides his cigars."

The best inspiration for getting a job done may be imagining how it will look once it is finished.

PLANTING THE PLAN

lorence Yoch (1890-1972), the gifted American landscape architect, made the following observation: "Gardens are not regarded to exist exclusively for the benefit of plants; but, rather that plants exist for gardens."

Implicit in that statement is the thought that backyards exist for people first, and for plants second. True, a backyard without plants would be a dismal sight, but one without people would have no reason to exist. Not everyone is interested in becoming an avid gardener, and not even those who *are* interested have the time. Still, you can have a beautiful backyard without becoming a slave to gardening.

The Selection Process

When it comes time to select plants for the backyard, most people start with a list of favorite plants. If you're looking for the least amount of upkeep, this is *not* the way to go about planting your backyard.

Every geographic and climatic region of the country has plants well-suited to its particular conditions. These are grasses, annuals, perennials, shrubs, vines, and trees that display an admirable willingness to grow. They may not be the most unusual plants; in fact, most of them will be quite common. But a common plant that is in thriving condition is far more attractive and easy to maintain than a rare plant that only limps along.

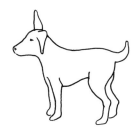

"More trees! More trees! What can I say? I'm a card-carrying member of the Urban Reforestation Program."

This is precisely what happened to a bachelor uncle of mine. After building his dream house, the one bit of "landscaping" he simply *had* to accomplish was the planting of a southern magnolia outside the French doors of his bedroom. He envisioned this elegant tree with their satiny flowers, pale in the moonlight, their heavy perfume drifting down into his chambers. But the magnolia of his dreams was so poorly suited to his climate, no local nursery carried the tree. Even the fact that he had to order it from a mail-order nursery a thousand miles from his home didn't deter him. Visiting him years after he planted the tree, I noticed the magnolia hadn't grown, and it was in very sad condition. Turning his back on the tree, my uncle bitterly complained, "That damn tree doesn't have the will to live, or the decency to die." Eventually, he tore the poor tree out.

The moral of the story is to stick with plants that are sure bets. In addition to choosing plants appropriate to your region, select individual plants well-suited to the exact location you intend to plant them. When you go to the nursery or garden center, know the exposure of each of your planting sites—does a particular site receive only morning sun, hot afternoon sun from 2 o'clock on, or dappled sunlight under a large deciduous tree? Explain the growing conditions to the salesperson, describe how big the area is, and then request to see appropriate plants for each specific area. When choosing trees or shrubs, select only those plants that will physically fit, when mature, into the

The All-Important First Step

*N*othing, repeat, nothing, is more important to the successful growth of plants than proper advance soil preparation. Skip this all-important first step and you're simply asking for trouble. Abide by it, and you've taken a huge step in insuring a thriving, easy-to-care-for garden.

Briefly stated, no matter what type of soil you find in your backyard, from the sandiest sand to the heaviest clay, a liberal addition of organic matter works miracles. The organic matter can be anything from compost to well-rotted leafmold, or fine fir bark to peat moss. Almost every area of the country lays claim to some indigenous, inexpensive organic material, readily available in bulk quantities from garden supply stores. Some communities even make compost available to homeowners for free, the material having been made from the leaves gathered by municipal crews in the fall.

The amount of organic matter to add should be equal to the depth that you intend to turn the soil. If you're preparing the soil to plant a lawn, whether it's from seed or sod, the minimum depth you should till is six inches; eight or twelve is that much better. This may contradict some traditional advice, but experience has proven it very successful. If you intend to till the soil to a depth of eight inches, then you should add eight inches of organic material on top of the soil before you till to incorporate it to the full depth. This takes some doing, but it helps develop an extensive, healthy root system, which results in a hardy, vigorous lawn, able to withstand periods of drought and more resistant to disease and pests.

The same holds true for shrub borders, flower beds, areas intended for groundcovers, and even vegetable gardens. Shrub borders and areas where groundcover is to be planted should be tilled to a depth of eight to twelve inches; flower beds and vegetable gardens, six to eight inches.

Depending on what you are planting and the characteristics of your native soil, you may want to add fertilizer and lime as you incorporate the organic matter. Explain your situation to your local nursery to find out if such additions are necessary.

After tilling the organic matter into the soil, rake the area smooth and plant your plants. Build small dikes around individual plants (roughly the diameter of the root ball), and keep them well-watered for the first few weeks after planting. In such superior soil, you'll be amazed at the growth they put on, even in the first year.

allotted space. This will all but eliminate pruning, and your plants will be allowed to achieve their natural form rather than some abstract Cubist shape resulting from repeated trimming.

If the plant selection process sounds like it takes a fair amount of research and effort, it does. But you don't have to be the one to go to the effort or do the research. Most reputable nurseries will provide you with a custom planting plan, usually free, if you agree to purchase the plants from their nursery. In most cases, this is a fair trade-off. Just make sure to let the salesperson know that you want plants with a marked willingness to grow in your location, and then leave the selection process in their capable hands.

Once the plants have been selected, how you plant them will have a significant effect on their ultimate performance. "Soil preparation" has an unglamorous ring to it, but when done correctly, it can help produce some very glamorous results (see *The All-Important First Step* at left). At the time you're improving the soil, it may seem to be nothing more than a lot of work, but no one step will pay off more handsomely in the long run. A plant that has to struggle to survive because of difficult soil conditions will grow slowly, lack vigor, be subject to attack from pests and diseases, and never quite meet your expectations. One of the most overlooked facts in gardening is that a healthy, vigorous plant will need next to no attention from the owner, while a weak plant will need more or less constant assistance in the form of sprays and assorted tonics.

A Case for Lawns

Much has been said and written about whether or not Americans should rethink their passion for the home lawn. There is general agreement that where summer rains are adequate and a well-adapted variety of grass is grown, lawns make perfect sense. Unfortunately, geographic areas where summer rains are adequate enough to support a lush, green stand of grass are few and far between in this country.

While acknowledging the validity of those points, there is no surface better suited to outdoor living and game-playing than a grass lawn. And no matter how much space you have, the bigger the lawn, the better! Period.

Shade Trees

High on the list of backyard priorities is at least one shade tree. Lucky is the person who inherits, along with the house, a beautiful, strategically located, mature shade tree. If you're not that lucky, the consolation is in being able to choose the type of tree you want, and planting it exactly where you want it.

Faced with a treeless backyard, the feature most people ask for when shopping for trees is anything "fast-growing." While this is perfectly understandable, beware. In virtually every part of the country, the fastest growing shade trees adapted to that area also have more than their fair share of drawbacks. For some, it is susceptibility to a regional disease. Others have weak limb structures that break easily in storms, and some trees are short-lived and go into decline shortly after they reach the size where they provide that much sought-after shade.

Before planting any shade tree, consult with your local nursery, garden center, or agricultural extension service. Ask for a list of recommended trees and find out as much as you can about their traits, both good and bad. In the long run, you may be better off with a slightly slower-growing tree, but one that will mature into a healthy, long-lived specimen.

And don't be lulled into thinking that just because a tree will take several years to mature, there's no rush to plant it. As my father always told me, "The sooner you get a tree planted, the sooner it can start to grow for you."

"I'll make a case for lawns. They're the perfect all-purpose surface, from Frisbee to...well, you know."

47

ENVIRONMENT-FRIENDLY LAWN CARE

BEFORE SEEDING OR SODDING A NEW LAWN, FOLLOW THE DIRECTIONS GIVEN IN "THE ALL-IMPORTANT FIRST STEP," FOUND ON PAGE 46. DON'T SKIMP ON THE ORGANIC MATTER!

NEVER CUT MORE THAN ONE-THIRD OF THE TOTAL HEIGHT OF YOUR GRASS. AND DON'T BAG YOUR CLIPPINGS. LET THEM FALL WHERE THEY MAY AND RETURN THEIR NITROGEN TO THE LAWN.

USE A FERTILIZER WITH NITROGEN FROM A NATURAL SOURCE, OR FROM UREAFORM, BOTH OF WHICH RESIST RAPID LEACHING FROM THE SOIL.

WHEN YOU WATER, WATER WELL. SHORT PERIODS OF WATERING ENCOURAGE SHALLOW ROOT SYSTEMS.

RELAX YOUR STANDARDS REGARDING WEEDS. LEARN TO LOVE DANDELIONS. IF YOU MUST SPRAY FOR WEEDS, PESTS, OR DISEASES, BY ALL MEANS FAVOR ENVIRONMENTALLY RESPONSIBLE PRODUCTS.

The most practical and thoughtful opinions have suggested that a lawn is well worth the energy and expense it requires, in any region of the country, if it is *actively* used as a surface for outdoor living and playing. If, however, you do not intend to use the lawn for game-playing and entertaining, by all means consider planting another type of groundcover, one well-adapted to your area. Once they are established, maintenance requirements for groundcovers are far less than for lawns. They make perfect sense when all that's required is an even visual expanse of green to fill-in the area between the house and the fence. Ask at your local nursery or garden center for a list of groundcover plants suitable for your area.

If you determine that a grass lawn makes sense your backyard, but you live in a climate ill-suited to supporting it naturally, there are four steps you can take to reduce its high maintenance requirements and all but eliminate any negative environmental impact.

Step Number One

First, instead of bagging the lawn clippings, let them compost in place, right on the lawn. Recent research has shown that leaving the clippings on the lawn is actually beneficial to the soil and the lawn. As the clippings decompose, they improve the structure of the soil and return nitrogen to the lawn.

The shorter the clippings, the more easily they fall to the soil (as opposed to lying on top of the grass), and the more quickly they decompose. Optimally, you should never cut more than one-third off the total height of the grass. This means you may need to mow your lawn on a slightly more frequent schedule, but it's a small price to pay for improving the health of your lawn while eliminating the effort involved in bagging and hauling clippings around the yard.

Step Number Two

Second, use a fertilizer with a nitrogen component that comes from a natural source, or ureaform, both of which release nitrogen slowly. Other forms of nitrogen may provide a quick green-up, but are so highly soluble much of the nitrogen is leached through the soil without the grass ever having a chance to use it. It is these soluble forms of nitrogen, such as ammonium nitrate, that have caused problems by polluting ground water and nearby streams and lakes.

Step Number Three

Third, relax your standards somewhat regarding what are seen as "weeds." It was no less than the great American horticulturist, Liberty Hyde Bailey, who wrote in 1898, "The man who worries morning and night about the dandelions in the lawn will find great relief in loving the dandelions. Each blossom is worth more than a gold coin, as it shimmers in the exuberant sunlight of the growing spring, and attracts the bees to its bosom. Little children love the dandelions: why may not we? Love the things nearest at hand; and love intensely."

Instead of trying to achieve that nearly impossible perfect grass lawn, completely free of dandelions, crabgrass, clover and whatnot, why not leave the herbicides on the shelf and simply mow what you've got? A lawn with a few weeds in it is not going to stop anyone from having a grand time playing touch football, badminton, or hide-and-seek. Leave perfection to the greenskeepers and their putting greens.

Step Number Four

Fourth, and finally, if insect pests become a serious problem, opt for a natural control. Great strides have been made in the science of organic pesticides. Today there is an effective, natural control product available for every lawn pest. These products make sense not only from an environmental point of view, but from a personal one as well. All one has to do is imagine the number of times kids fall face-down in the grass during an active game of volleyball or football, or just how close to the lawn babies or toddlers are as they crawl or wobble across the grass, and the choice of insect remedies becomes very clear-cut.

Branching Out

In the initial planting phase, you are simply trying to establish the "backbone" of the garden. The time to experiment with unusual or hard-to-grow plants is *after* the shade trees and the sure-bet, backbone plantings have become established. If the experimental plantings don't work out, at least the backbone of your backyard plantings will still be there, looking great. But don't give up experimenting.

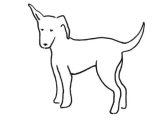

"Keep that smelly stuff off my lawn, please! Just licking my paws after being out there makes me sick."

WATER GARDENS

NATURALISTIC-LOOKING PONDS CAN TAKE ANY SHAPE YOU DESIRE. LARGE ROCKS AND WATER-LOVING PLANTS AT THE EDGES OF THE POND WILL GO A LONG WAY IN CREATING A REALISTIC SCENE.

WHERE SPACE IS CRAMPED, WALL FOUNTAINS ARE JUST THE TICKET. TAKING UP ALMOST NO SPACE AT ALL, THEY NONETHELESS PROVIDE THE SIGHT AND SOUND OF FALLING WATER—VERY PLEASANT, INDEED.

FORMAL PONDS ARE BUILT IN GEOMETRIC SHAPES—CIRCLES, SQUARES, RECTANGLES, OR OCTAGONS. TO COMPLEMENT THEIR FORMALITY, THEY SHOULD BE PLACED SYMMETRICALLY, RATHER THAN CASUALLY OFF-CENTER IN THE SPACE THEY OCCUPY.

SOME OF THE MOST CHARMING OF ALL WATER FEATURES HAVE THEIR ROOTS IN JAPAN. THE GENTLE DRIP OF WATER FROM A BAMBOO PIPE INTO A MOSS-COVERED STONE BOWL IS A RARE AND ENGAGING SIGHT.

Experimenting with plants you've never grown before and watching your garden evolve from one season to the next are two traits that make gardening such a compelling hobby, and backyards such a nice place to be.

It's comforting to remember that the living component of your backyard—the "green" part—is something that is meant to evolve over time. Don't be surprised that with each passing year, the look of your yard will change, sometimes dramatically. You may find the lawn dying out under your maturing shade trees, demanding a shade-tolerant groundcover instead of grass. A shrub that was supposed to grow only four feet tall may grow to seven, crowding out its neighbor. And after years of worrying about planting thorny, bee-attracting roses next to the baby's sandbox, you find yourself with a teenager on your hands and a sandbox converted to a planter filled with floribundas. Who knows? Maybe after a few years of experimenting with this plant or that, you may find yourself actually enjoying work in the garden.

Hobby Gardens

The best thing about a backyard with low-maintenance plantings is that it leaves you free to pursue other interests. Ironically, one of those other interests may be gardening. If you're scratching your head right now, that statement is not meant to be a conundrum. It's just that a big yard, full of high-maintenance plantings, is simply overwhelming to many people. But when high-maintenance plantings are restricted to a small, separate, defined area, they're much easier to manage—a leisure-time hobby, rather than a demanding chore.

Most hobbies, of any sort, have many dimensions. That's what makes a hobby interesting and worth pursuing. The following five types of gardens—water gardens, kitchen gardens, herb gardens, cutting gardens, and rose gardens—fall easily into the hobby category. Each has a long, rich history and unique plants that lead to use in a variety of crafts and activities beyond the garden. The rewards offered by this type of speciality gardens are disproportionate to the size you can devote to them: No matter how small, the enjoyment and satisfaction can be great.

Water Gardens

Florence Yoch, the brilliant landscape architect quoted at the beginning of this chapter, had this to say about water gardens: "Water is always essential and is by far the most interesting feature in any garden."

Although it has been many years since a fountain or pool was considered a garden "essential," more and more people are discovering the joys of water gardening, so much so that it has become the fastest-growing type of gardening in America today. Because of its increasing popularity, there is now a wide variety of options in water gardening, and they are more widely available than at any time in the past.

Fountains and ponds are the most common way of adding water to a landscape, but even something as simple as a birdbath adds a little of water's reflective charm to the garden, while at the same time doing something nice for the birds. Another simple way to add water in a garden setting, seldom seen anymore, is with a dipping well. Dipping wells must be filled from a hose, but what they lack in practicality, they make up for in charm. Anything from an old wellhead, a large porcelain pot, a stone or cast-concrete trough, or a large rock with a hollowed-out basin to hold the water can be used as a dipping well. With a long-handled dipper nearby, the dipping well can be used for watering container plants and as a place to wash off your hands or bare feet. Birds undoubtedly will find their way to the dipping well, and thank you for your thoughtfulness with frequent patronage.

If you decide on a fountain or pool, the type you choose is largely a matter of personal preference and the opportunities afforded by your yard. There are wonderful terra cotta and cast wall fountains that come complete with recirculating pumps. Vinyl liners are available in many shapes and depths, which make installing a pool almost as easy as digging a hole (for more information, see pages 122-123). And there's always the option of a custom designed pool, formed from poured concrete. There are few hard-and-fast rules regarding fountain and pool styles, with the exception that formal (geometrically shaped) pools look best in formal gardens, and pools and waterfalls of natural (free-form) designs are best suited to informal yards.

Whatever you choose, take advantage of a fountain's magnetic charms and place it in an alluring location. Foun-

Fish for Your Pond

If you have a pond, you definitely should have fish. They are the final touch that brings the pond to life. Either goldfish or koi, both members of the carp family, are the best bets. Most aquarium fish are too fragile, and wild fish are too destructive to plants. Fish can be ordered from mail-order water garden catalogs (yes, they do ship live fish through the mail— see pages 122-123 for sources) or from most local pet shops.

As exotic as they appear, goldfish and koi are remarkably hardy and long-lived. They can fend for themselves while you are on vacation, and once they become used to your presence, they can even be taught to do tricks. The easiest trick to teach them is to eat from your hand, but with a little patience they can be trained to jump through hoops, drink from a baby bottle, or even puff on a cigar!

"Those fish don't do much for me, but I would like to see that cigar trick!"

KITCHEN GARDENS

KITCHEN GARDENS, LAID OUT IN A FORMAL STYLE, ARE DESCENDENTS OF THE *POTAGERS* OF FRANCE. EQUALLY AT HOME ADJOINING A GRAND CHATEAU OR A HUMBLE COTTAGE, THE GROWING OF VEGETABLES IN AN AESTHETICALLY PLEASING MANNER GIVES GREAT PRIDE TO FRENCH GARDENERS.

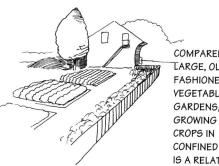

COMPARED TO LARGE, OLD-FASHIONED VEGETABLE GARDENS, GROWING FOOD CROPS IN CONFINED BEDS IS A RELATIVELY SIMPLE PROPOSITION. IN FACT, YOU MAY FIND IT SO EASY AND REWARDING, YOU'LL WANT MORE THAN ONE BED.

WHY NOT BUILD A LITTLE VEGETABLE-CLEANING STATION IN YOUR SIDEYARD, CLOSE TO THE KITCHEN GARDEN. DIRT AND TRIMMINGS CAN BE DISPOSED OF EASILY. YOU MAY ALSO FIND IT A HANDY PLACE TO CLEAN FISH, PREPARE FLOWER ARRANGEMENTS, OR FOR HOSING DOWN KIDS AND PETS AFTER A ROMP IN THE MUD.

tains make wonderful "eye-catchers" at the far end of a view across a garden, sure to inspire visitors to walk the full length of your yard. If you want to grow water plants, including any of the wonderful waterlilies or lotuses, locate the pool where it will receive at least six hours of sunlight a day.

Goldfish and koi are natural inhabitants of water gardens, adding an exotic shimmer of life beneath the water's surface. In areas where raccoons are prevalent, you may have to take some precautions against their using your pool as a fishing hole. Both goldfish and koi live for decades and can dwell year-round in your pool, even in cold winter climates, provided the pool is outfitted with a simple, electric pool heater.

Natural-looking, free-form pools lend themselves well to natural plantings around the edges. Catalogs that specialize in water gardening have recently begun stocking a good selection of "bog" plants, which are really quite unlike any other plants normally seen in most gardens (see pages 122-123). Whether it is a gunnera plant, which grows to eight feet tall with leaves between 4- and 8-feet across, the horsetail rush, with its 4-foot-tall skinny stems and umbrella-like foliage, or any of the other exotic bog-lovers, these plants are sure to inspire comment.

Water gardens are rewarding in many ways. Best of all may be the magical way they bring a garden to life, inviting even the most harried and preoccupied person to sit a moment and reflect at the water's edge. Although it may seem like an extravagant extra, give serious consideration to adding a water garden in your backyard plans. You may not get to constructing it this year or next. But when you do, you'll have only one regret—that you didn't build it sooner.

Kitchen Gardens

If you enjoy cooking, there's nothing quite so satisfying as being able to step out your back door to grab that bit of parsley or basil you need for a pot of simmering soup, pick a few of your favorite hot peppers to spice up a salsa, or slice into that first eagerly-awaited, vine-ripened tomato. While the old-fashioned, rambling vegetable garden may be hard to fit into most of today's small backyards—not to mention hard to fit into your schedule—a small kitchen garden of herbs, vegetables, and flowers can easily fit into almost any backyard and be a delight, rather than a pain, to maintain.

Kitchen gardens (or as the French call them, *potagers*) are directly related to the cloistered gardens in medieval monasteries. In essence, the cloistered garden was a garden of choice, useful plants, located close-at-hand, given special attention and protection by the cloister walls. The plants included many herbs, a few vegetables, and a variety of flowering plants used for medicinal purposes. Because of the interesting combination of plants, and the fact that they received close, daily attention, these were attractive small plots, admired as much for their beauty as their culinary contributions.

Today's kitchen gardens have retained their double artful/edible personality. Typically laid out in a square planting bed, say 10 by 10 feet, they are often neatly edged with a low boxwood hedge. The square bed is divided into four symmetrical beds (each 60 inches square), and filled with vegetables, herbs and a few flowers, designed and planted with an eye toward beauty as well as produce for the kitchen table. Neat patterns of different colored lettuces create a tapestry effect, green onion tops march in military precision, and four string bean-covered teepees mark the outside corners of the garden. As a crowning touch, a sundial, birdbath, or gazing ball can be placed in the center of the garden, perhaps surrounded by those heavenly blue flowers of the borage plant and orange nasturtiums. The flowers of both plants are edible and make wonderful additions to salads.

Plant your kitchen garden where it will receive at least six hours of sunlight each day and as close to the kitchen as possible. Before planting, prepare the soil as outlined on page 46. Limit the vegetables and herbs to those that you really enjoy using on a regular basis and, whenever possible, plant dwarf or compact varieties of standard vegetables for the most efficient use of space.

Herb Gardens

More than a few people with only a passing interest in cooking or gardening have found themselves fascinated with the growing and using of herbs. It's not all that surprising, because, as a group, herbs may well be the most intriguing of all plants to grow. Complementing their unique flavors, virtually every herb grown today has its own complex history and a fascinating legacy of folklore. Start with a single plant

HERB GARDENS

A NEATLY ARRANGED, TRIMMED HERB GARDEN RIGHT NEAR THE HOUSE CAN BE AS ATTRACTIVE AS IT IS USEFUL. DWARF BOXWOOD MAKES A GOOD-LOOKING BORDER. ADD A FEW FLOWERING ANNUALS FOR COLOR, IF YOU LIKE, ESPECIALLY THOSE WITH EDIBLE FLOWERS.

IF YOU DECIDE TO PLANT CATNIP AS A TREAT FOR YOUR FAMILY PET, BE PREPARED FOR PLENTY OF FELINE VISITORS TO YOUR GARDEN. THEY GO FOR THIS STUFF IN SHAMELESS ABANDON.

A FREE-STANDING HERB GARDEN, BORDERED WITH STONE OR BRICK, MAKES A NICE SPOT TO PLACE A BIRDBATH. ONCE THE HERBS BLOOM, AND THE BEES AND BUTTERFLIES DISCOVER THEM, YOU'LL HAVE A MINIATURE WILDLIFE PRESERVE.

"Planted plenty of catnip for those cats…what do you mean you've never heard of 'dognip'?"

CUTTING GARDENS

THERE'S NO NEED TO ARRANGE FLOWERING PLANTS ATTRACTIVELY IN CUTTING GARDENS. JUST LAYING THE PLANTS OUT IN STRAIGHT ROWS, OR IN NARROW RAISED BEDS, WILL DO NICELY, MAKING IT EASY TO TEND AND CUT THE FLOWERS.

A NARROW, DEEP BUCKET, AVAILABLE AT FLORISTS AND SOME NURSERIES, IS IDEAL FOR CUT FLOWERS. FILL IT WITH WATER AND TAKE RIGHT INTO THE GARDEN. FOR LONG-LIVED CUT FLOWERS, PLUNGE THEM IN THE WATER AS SOON AS THEY'RE CUT.

A SHARP PAIR OF SHEARS IS ESSENTIAL FOR MAKING CLEAN CUTS. CRUSHED OR DAMAGED STEMS INVITE DECAY AND SHORTEN THE LIFE OF CUT FLOWERS.

THE BEST TIME TO CUT FLOWERS IS IN THE MORNING, WHEN THE LEAVES AND STEMS ARE FULL OF WATER. DON'T WAIT UNTIL THE AFTERNOON, WHEN THE PLANTS ARE OFTEN WILTED.

of parsley, and in a couple of seasons you may find yourself hooked on growing every type of herb you can lay your hands on.

It's easy to create a small herb garden, and very rewarding. A space as small as a 5- by 5-foot plot is ample for a good sampling of herbs. Many of our favorite herbs are from the sunny Mediterranean region and grow naturally in gravelly, lean soil. Make your herb plants feel right at home by planting the bed in full sun and filling it with a fast-draining soil. If the soil is naturally heavy, add a few bags of sand to the plot and turn it into the top six or eight inches of soil. Add fertilizer sparingly, if at all. It's a good idea to label the herb plants to help those who might be unfamiliar with what they look like—such as young children—should they ever be sent out to garden to gather a little of this or that for the evening meal.

You can plant the herbs in whatever arrangement pleases you, formal or informal. Some gardeners take special enjoyment from planting intricate, living patterns with their herb plants, using dwarf, small-leaved basil plants to create fast-growing green boundaries between the various herbs, much like a little clipped boxwood hedge.

Once you've experienced the joy of having fresh herbs close at hand, they will surely become a permanent part of your backyard.

Cutting Gardens

Many people who have flowers growing in their yards are reluctant to cut them, for fear that they'll diminish the beauty of the display. If you like cut flowers, the easiest way to ensure a ready supply for arrangements—without denuding the border next to the lawn—is to plant a cutting garden. It's a rather old-fashioned notion, but one well worth reviving.

It helps to think of a cutting garden as a utilitarian type of garden, not unlike a plot of vegetables. Hidden away in a side yard, behind a fence, or in a far corner of your backyard, you're free to plant flowers for cutting in practical rows, rather than trying to create aesthetically pleasing combinations, as you might if the bed were on public display. And just like a vegetable garden, make sure there are paths between the rows to permit easy maintenance and cutting.

One of the best ways to construct a cutting garden is with raised beds. With sides built of 2 x 4's or 2 x 6's, watering and weeding are more easily accomplished, and improving the soil within the beds can be more done more effectively.

The choice of which flowers to plant is, of course, up to you, but plant at least some annuals. They come into flower quickly after planting, have a long blooming season, and best of all, the more you cut them, the more they bloom. Annuals such as marigolds, zinnias, ageratum, snapdragons, and stock are available in both dwarf and standard forms. The standard or tall forms will provide long stems for cutting.

Flowers should be cut just as they fully open, preferably in the morning when they are fresh and full of moisture. When cutting flowers, take a deep bucket of water into the garden and submerge the entire stem of the flower as soon as it is cut. Many professional flower arrangers recommend cutting the stems a second time with a sharp knife, underwater, before arranging. This prevents a bubble of air from forming in the stem of the flower, permitting a free flow of water and the longest possible life.

Roses—All-Time Favorites

With their great beauty, tremendous variety, and luscious scent, it's easy to become passionate about roses. For many, roses are the very symbol of a well-cared-for home, evoking images of that picket-fenced cottage awash with rambling roses. Like Oscar Wilde, who could "resist anything except temptation," the rewards are rich for those who give in to the temptation of roses. In addition to beautiful flowers for arrangements, roses lend themselves to a wide variety of crafts—everything from petals for creating potpourri, to the vitamin C-rich seed pods (called rose hips) for rose hip tea.

If you decide to plant a rose *garden*, do it with the understanding that, as with all temptations, there will be a price to pay. To do what they do so well—namely, produce quantities of beautiful, fragrant flowers—roses need special attention. And although it's possible to mix any number of roses in with a shrub border, its's far easier to be lavish with that attention if they are segregated in a small bed. Ten to twelve rose bushes will make a magnificent display, provide plenty of flowers for cutting, and require a bed only eight by twelve feet or so. Any shape of bed will do, but generations of gardeners have favored the formal look of square,

Finding That *One* Rose

It's not unusual for roses to become the object of something close to fanaticism. In situations of passionate interest, there's nothing more frustrating than trying to locate that one rose you simply must have—especially when that one rose proves elusive. Relief can be found in the form of The Combined Rose List, *a paperback book published every year.* The Combined Rose List *contains the name and source for virtually every rose in commerce in the United States and Canada, as well as some foreign sources. Ask for* The Combined Rose List *at your local library, or write to Peter Schneider, P. O. Box 16035, Rocky River, Ohio 44116, to request ordering information.*

"'A rose is a rose is a...' What is it about roses, anyway? I think Gertrude was onto something."

55

ROSE GARDENS

A SMALL BED OF ROSES, PLANTED WITH SEVERAL DIFFERENT VARIETIES, WILL OFFER A GREAT DEAL OF ENJOYMENT TO THE ROSE FANCIER, WITHOUT MAKING UNDUE DEMANDS OF TIME AND ATTEN-TION.

BE SURE AND PICK THE ROSES THAT GROW MOST READILY IN YOUR AREA.

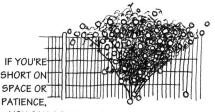

THE NARROW STRIP BETWEEN A DRIVEWAY AND LAWN MAKES AN IDEAL SPOT FOR ROSES, PLANTED SINGLE FILE. ADD LOW-GROWING, FLOWERING PLANTS AT THE EDGES, AND YOU'LL HAVE AN ATTRACTIVE, EASY TO MAINTAIN FLOWER GARDEN.

MANY PEOPLE GROW ROSES JUST FOR USING IN BOUQUETS. IF THIS IS YOUR AIM, FAVOR THE HYBRID TEAS, WITH THEIR LONG SEASON OF BLOOM.

IF YOU'RE SHORT ON SPACE OR PATIENCE, YOU CAN AT LEAST HAVE ONE RAMBLING ROSE PLANTED AGAINST YOUR FENCE. IT WILL PAY RICH REWARDS FOR A VERY SMALL INVESTMENT.

rectangular, or round beds, edged with stone or brick, often with a birdbath or sundial placed in the center for a little added interest.

If you want maximum return on your bed of roses, four important requirements should be taken into consideration: 1) selection of the rose varieties, 2) location of the planting bed, 3) soil preparation, and 4) consistent care.

When choosing roses, always favor those adapted to your growing region. Consult local gardening authorities—your neighborhood nursery, extension agent, or garden club—for a list of roses that grow well in your area. The list may not contain all (or *any*, for that matter) of your favorites, but there will be plenty to choose from, some of which are bound to become new favorites. The selection process is a very important step in the creation of a successful rose garden. By choosing naturally vigorous roses that are suited to your climate, the amount of care they require will dramatically decrease.

A small bed of roses can function as the focal point of a backyard, but don't let design considerations blind you to the rose's specific needs. In the main, roses require a sunny location, at least six hours per day. Ideally, the location should provide good air circulation and receive morning sun to help dry off leaves early in the day. Too much shade encourages disease problems. If the shade is produced by mature trees, their extensive root systems will rob nutrients from the roses, a situation that results in few flowers and weak plants. And if there are youngsters in your household, take care to locate the rose bed where an errant football or Frisbee isn't likely to wreak havoc.

Once you have outlined the shape of the rose bed, it's time to improve the soil—*before* planting the roses. Because they are rather finicky about soil, it's a good idea to have your soil tested. Some large nurseries and most university extension services will do this for a nominal charge. Once your soil analysis is complete, you will know exactly what should be added to the soil and in what amount. This is not the time for skimping. Any extra effort you put into advance preparation will pay off in superior results for years to come.

Standard care includes watering, fertilizing, protecting against pests and diseases, and pruning. Roses need regular applications of water for top production of flowers. It makes no difference whether the water is applied from a hose or from rain. Just make sure they receive enough water to moisten the soil to a depth of 18 inches every week during the growing season. The easiest way to check this is with a long screwdriver or stiff piece of wire, such as a straightened-out coat hanger It will be easy to push through moist soil, more difficult once it hits dry soil. In arid summer climates, consider watering your roses with a drip system that is connected to a timer.

At least two applications of fertilizer should be made, once when new growth first starts in the spring and again in mid-season. Favor non-burning, natural formulations that feed the soil as well as the plant.

Vigorously growing roses will be far less susceptible to attack from pests and diseases than those that are struggling. There are effective natural controls for virtually every pest known to plague roses (see pages 122-123). If you know of diseases that are a problem in your area (such as black spot, rust, and mildew), use a natural fungicide to combat the problem *before* it occurs. Diseases are impossible to eradicate once they make an appearance, although they *can* be stopped from doing additional damage.

Don't be surprised if any of the aforementioned hobby gardens turns into a full-blown passion. That's the way it is with plants and the people who love them. The gardening bug doesn't bite everyone, but once bitten, it's one of the most delightful maladies any backyard has to offer.

Flowers in Containers

People sometimes talk about their container-grown plants as "pets." And like pets, they require regular care and attention—not much, mind you, but regular. In exchange, a few containers planted with flowering shrubs, annuals, or perennials will offer the colorful impact of a much larger bed or border for a fraction of the work. Don't be afraid to experiment with plants not normally grown in containers. Virtually any plant (including roses) can be grown in a pot, provided it receives the proper care.

Make it easy on yourself, and fill your containers with any of the packaged, light-weight soil mixes sold in nurseries and garden centers. While you're at it, pick up some "timed" or "slow-release" fertilizer. One application at planting time should just about take care of the plant's nutrient needs for an entire growing season. Read and follow the label directions. If you notice the plants waning late in the season (symptoms include yellowing leaves and fewer flowers), make a second application of fertilizer.

Aside from using a good soil mix and making sure there are enough nutrients available, don't forget to water your container-grown plants on a regular basis. During hot, dry weather, they will need a good soaking every day. And if you're leaving home for even one summer weekend, have someone water the container plants for you.

"Make sure that the clown who waters the flowers remembers to give me some water, too."

Few cultures have paid as much attention to refinement and details as the Japanese. Stone basins, this one cloaked in a velvety layer of moss, are traditionally placed in tea gardens. Their low stature forces visitors to stop and crouch while washing their hands, a gesture that inspires a moment of reflection and, hopefully, appreciation.

ACS
1991

"GOD IS IN THE DETAILS"

I t was the famous modern architect, Mies van der Rohe, who coined the statement, "God is in the details." As anyone who has ever tackled a large project knows, it takes true spirit and an inspired vision to see the work through to the minutest detail. Once the big construction projects—the fences, gates, patios, decks, arbors, and walkways—have been completed, and the backyard is planted the way you want it, the time finally comes to focus in on a few details. Some of the details may be so small you might think you're doing them only for yourself. But any sensitive soul who passes through your private retreat is sure to appreciate the totality of your creation, sensing a little of the person and the vision behind it.

Getting to the point where the details matter takes time. I recall one friend who said he looked forward to the day when he could put one of those miniature bamboo rakes to good use, gingerly removing the fallen leaves and litter from between well-grown shrubs. That diminutive rake represented a world to him, where instead of having to tackle the monumental jobs in his yard, and perhaps his life, he would be able to slow down and savor the details. Perhaps the details themselves are less important than what they represent: the arrival of a time when refinement matters.

Backyard details include everything from practicalities such as furniture and lighting to quixotic items such as that bamboo rake, statues, ornamental water spigots, hand-carved hose-guards, or even a beautifully crafted rope ladder for that tree house.

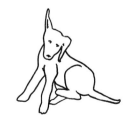

"As a Zen master once said, 'What else is there, besides details?'"

59

Furniture

As outdoor living becomes second nature to more and more people, a greater selection of outdoor furniture is being made available. There are beautiful wood chairs, chaises and tables made in traditional designs, wicker furniture, metal and wrought iron pieces good for several generations of use, canvas and wood umbrellas big enough to shield a crowd during a sudden shower, hammocks made from rope or old-fashioned canvas, and all kinds of new, "miracle" fabrics for outdoor upholstery that resist the damaging effects of the sun and extreme weather conditions.

You can adopt a casual attitude (epitomized by the European penchant for using old kitchen tables surrounded by a motley assortment of chairs) or a studied approach that dictates strict adherence to one particular style of furniture. Just remember that the backyard is meant to be enjoyed with abandon. Instead of making a big design statement, it's okay to err on the side of charm and informality.

Comfort and durability should be your first two concerns for outdoor furniture. Some of the most attractive chairs can be hideously uncomfortable. If you're ordering furniture from a catalog, it's not a bad idea to search out a local showroom where you can do to a little comfort testing before ordering something "sight un-sat-in." When it comes to durability, keep in mind that outdoor furniture must stand up to all types of weather, as well as considerable punishment from kids, dogs, spilled drinks, and being hauled around from one end of the yard to the other.

Outdoor tables should be as big as they come, and definitely bigger than you think you need at the time. A big outdoor table is ideal for casual group dinners, for many more people than you could or would invite over for a dinner party indoors. When spread with newspapers or a plastic tablecloth, a huge table is also a wonderful place to do art, crafts and assorted building projects—not to mention the perfect place to hold kids' birthday parties. After any messy activity, clean-up is a simple process of hosing off the table and the "floor" at same time. Try *that* indoors!

The most flexible seating around any outdoor table is a pair of benches. But after sitting for a while, some people may complain about the lack of back support. If so, consider combining a few chairs with the benches. Set them at the ends of the table and offer them as places of honor to any that request them. Just because you're outdoors, it doesn't mean that everyone can't be comfortable.

The Adirondack chair is a timeless classic, and for good reason: comfort, room for food, drink, and reading material, as well as the fact that its design fosters good posture!

FURNITURE

METAL FURNITURE IS AVAILABLE IN CAST AND WROUGHT IRON, AS WELL AS ALUMINUM. ALTHOUGH THEY MAY APPEAR TO BE UNCOMFORTABLE AT FIRST GLANCE, MOST HAVE BEEN DESIGNED WITH THE HUMAN FORM IN MIND. IN A PINCH, CUSHIONS WILL WORK WONDERS.

RECENT YEARS HAVE SEEN THE RETURN OF CLASSIC WOODEN BENCH DESIGNS, MANY OF WHICH QUALIFY AS WORKS OF ART. AVAILABLE IN A VARIETY OF WOODS, FROM TEAK TO REDWOOD, ALL ARE CHOSEN WITH LONGEVITY AND WEATHER-RESISTANCE IN MIND.

ALMOST UNBELIEVABLY INEXPENSIVE, HUGE CHINESE MARKET UMBRELLAS ARE JUST THE THING WHEN YOU NEED A LOT OF SHADE IN A HURRY. MADE FROM BAMBOO AND OILED PAPER, THEY WILL LAST FOR SEVERAL SEASONS, WITH A LITTLE CARE.

A FEW CANVAS AND WOOD SLING-BACK CHAIRS GROUPED AROUND AN UMBRELLA CONSTITUTE A COMFORTABLE OUTDOOR GATHERING PLACE.

AS GREAT AS ROCKING CHAIRS ARE INDOORS, THEY'RE EVEN BETTER OUTDOORS. HANDSOME, TRADITIONAL DESIGNS ARE ONCE AGAIN BEING MADE FROM A VARIETY OF WEATHER-RESISTANT WOODS.

A RUSTIC PICNIC TABLE AND A PAIR OF MATCHING BENCHES ARE ABOUT AS UTILITARIAN AS OUTDOOR FURNITURE GETS. PRACTICALLY INDESTRUCTIBLE, THEY WILL PROVIDE MANY YEARS OF SERVICE WITH VIRTUALLY NO MAINTENANCE.

"I'm particularly fond of that Adirondack chair over there but, apparently, so is everyone else."

61

Lighting

As night falls in your backyard, some type of lighting will become a necessity—for safety as well as aesthetics. Just remember that a little lighting goes a long way. It is far better to be discreet than to have to shield your eyes from the glare of a misplaced or too-bright light.

Low-voltage lighting systems provide just the right amount of lighting for most backyard situations. New technology has revolutionized this type of lighting, bringing it well within the installation abilities of even novice do-it-yourselfers. Modular systems and kits are so inexpensive and easy to install that outdoor lighting is finally within the reach of everyone who wants it (see pages 122-123).

When you get ready to install your system, by all means wait until after dark to experiment with placing the lights in different locations. Although they are easy to move, there's no point in making extra work for yourself. Small trees, shrubs, walls, fences, and the outside of your house look best up-lit—that is, with the light source placed on the ground, pointing up, for a gentle wash of light. Mature trees can be effectively up-lit, too, but the light fixture should be placed up in the tree, rather than at the base of the trunk. This produces a gentle, glowing quality, very pleasant to sit under or view from across the yard.

For the sake of safety, walkways, steps, and edges of decks, patios, and terraces should be lit at night. Special fixtures are available for this purpose and are easy to install.

The light provided by paper Chinese lanterns may not be as practical as other outdoor lighting systems, but it is about as exotic and evocative as anything can be. These classic and inexpensive paper lanterns are available from variety and party-goods stores, and from some mail-order catalogs (see pages 122-123). Put a little sand in the bottom of each lantern, nestle a long-burning votive candle into the sand, light, hang from an overhanging tree limb, and let the magic they cast hold you in its sway.

If for some reason, you can't find any Chinese lanterns, you needn't be without the special effects of candlelight in your backyard. Luminaries, lunch-sized paper bags filled with a couple of inches of sand, are a great alternative to lanterns. They must be put on the ground instead of hung from trees, but they're ideal for marking a pathway, steps, for ringing the perimeter of an outdoor eating area or for lining up at the edge of an outdoor "stage." Brown paper bags work fine; white or yellow bags are even better. If you use short votive candles, you won't ever have any problem with the bag accidentally catching fire, even in the fiercest of winds. Once it burns to the quick, the flame will automatically extinguish itself in the sand.

If there's something more magical than candle-lit Chinese lanterns on a summer night, it's yet to be invented.

LIGHTING

HERE'S ONE I BET YOU HAVEN'T SEEN—MIDWESTERN PARTY LIGHTS. START BY ATTACHING A ROCK TO A LONG LENGTH OF HEAVY STRING OR CORD. THROW THE ROCK OVER THE TOP OF THE TREE. (MAKE SURE THE ROCK DOESN'T HIT ANYTHING—OR ANYONE—ON THE OTHER SIDE OF THE TREE. ATTACH A LONG LENGTH OF CHRISTMAS TREE LIGHTS TO THE ROCKLESS END OF THE STRING. PULL THE LIGHTS INTO THE TREE FROM THE ROCK-END OF THE STRING, STOPPING BEFORE THE LIGHTS GET TANGLED IN THE BRANCHES. WEIGHT AS MANY STRANDS OF LIGHTS AS YOU WANT AT THE GROUND END. REMOVAL IS EASY. SIMPLY CUT THE STRING AND PULL THE STRANDS OF LIGHTS FROM THE TREE.

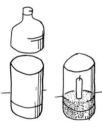

HURRICANE LAMPS IN A HURRY: THOSE TALL PLASTIC BOTTLES MINERAL WATER COMES IN MAKE PERFECT SUBSTITUTES FOR GLASS CHIMNEYS. CUT OFF THE TOP, FILL THE BOTTOM WITH SAND, AND ADD A SHORT CANDLE. LET THERE BE LIGHT—EVEN IN A GALE!

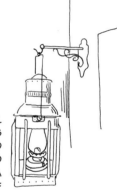

SEVERAL MANUFACTURERS HAVE RE-CREATED OLD-FASHIONED LANTERNS IN A VARIETY OF STYLES. AS CHARMING AS THEY APPEAR, MOST ARE ALSO QUITE EFFECTIVE AT DISPERSING LIGHT.

PAPER BAGS, FILLED WITH A FEW INCHES OF SAND AND A VOTIVE CANDLE ARE CALLED LUMINARIES. THEY'RE THE PERFECT THING FOR LINING THE ENTRANCE TO A BACKYARD PARTY, OR FOR HIGHLIGHTING STAIRS.

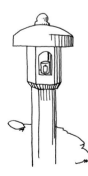

IT MAY BE HARD TO BELIEVE, BUT THERE ARE PEOPLE IN THIS COUNTRY WHO HAND-CARVE STONE GARDEN LANTERNS. UNDERSTANDABLY DEAR, THEY REPRESENT A LIFETIME INVESTMENT IN AN EVOCATIVE, TIMELESS FORM OF LIGHTING.

"Why all this trouble over lighting? Even a cat can see around the yard at night."

Ornament

From Cecile Matschat's *Planning the Home Grounds*, published in 1937, comes the following pointed advice: "Simple and dignified accessories give style and charm to any garden. Cast-iron dogs and deer are no longer considered in good taste." Now I admire simplicity as much as the next person, but *dignity*? Leave that to visiting heads of state (that's why they're called *dignitaries*). If you want to put that cast-iron spaniel in the middle of your lawn, why not?

In addition to cast-iron dogs, yard ornaments include everything from statuary, wall plaques, sundials, birdbaths, antique wheelbarrows, flags, tilework, plastic trolls, and gazing balls (or "witches' balls," as they are called in some parts of the country). It might also include treillage (a *very* tasteful and refined version of trelliswork, often designed to fool the eye—that would be *trompe l'oeil* in French—using tricks of forced perspective).

Virtually every home and garden designer in the world would say that it is possible to use too much ornament, telling anyone who might ask: "By all means limit yourself to one major 'eye-catcher,' and leave the rest on the showroom floor."

Four seasons in a gazing ball. Neither rain, nor sleet, nor blinding sun can keep these curiosities from reflecting the world around them.

Tasteful advice, to be sure, but some of the most charming backyards I've ever been in have had one concrete *tschochke* after another, peering out from the astilbes, or hiding behind the rhubarb patch. Too much, by far, for most people. But when it's an accurate reflection of what pleases the owner, it's just right.

Tradition, rather than taste, offers a few guidelines for the unsure: An imposing piece of statuary or a huge Chinese garden urn from the Hoo-Hoo dynasty—these are important ornaments that need to be highlighted. Place them at the end of a sightline—at the far end of a lawn, the termination of a walkway, or at the end of a "tunnel" of trees. A more modest ornament, perhaps a sundial or bird bath, is good for giving a geometrically shaped bed a focal point. It should be placed directly in the center of the bed. These suggestions have been followed since people first began making gardens, and they continue to produce desirable results.

A word of warning: If you have any old or valuable pieces of statuary in public view, make sure that they are very securely anchored. A recent surge of interest in "antique" garden ornament has lead to increased value and, unfortunately, theft.

ORNAMENT

A WEATHER VANE MAY NOT BE THE MOST PRACTICAL METHOD FOR DETERMINING TOMORROW'S FORECAST, BUT IT CERTAINLY ADDS A NOTE OF INTEREST TO THE PEAK OF ANY ROOF—EVEN THE ONE ON A GARDEN SHED.

TERRA-COTTA OR CAST CONCRETE WALL PLAQUES AND PLANTERS ARE NICE DETAILS, ESPECIALLY WHEN THEY CAN BE VIEWED UP CLOSE. CONSIDER PLACING THEM NEXT TO A DOOR OR GATE WHERE THEY CAN BE SUITABLY APPRECIATED.

GARDEN TROLLS ARE THE ABSOLUTE NADIR OF TASTE FOR SOME, THE VERY PICTURE OF CHARM FOR OTHERS. DUE TO A WORLDWIDE EPIDEMIC OF GOOD TASTE, THESE BRIGHTLY PAINTED TROLLS ARE BECOMING AS HARD TO FIND AS THEIR MYTHICAL SELVES. IMPORTED FROM EUROPE AND AVAILABLE IN VIRTUALLY EVERY CONCEIVABLE STANCE AND ACTIVITY, THEY CAN STILL BE FOUND, HERE AND THERE, IN NURSERIES AND GARDEN SHOPS.

USUALLY CAST IN BRONZE, SPIGOT ORNAMENTS TURN AN ATTRACTIVE VERDIGRIS OVER TIME. EVERY TIME YOU TURN THE WATER SPIGOT ON OR OFF, YOU GET TO ENJOY THE SIGHT AND FEEL OF A MINOR PIECE OF SCULPTURE.

A VICTORIAN HEAT REGISTER COVER MAKES THE PERFECT PEEP-HOLE. FIND THEM AT YOUR LOCAL ARCHITECTURAL SALVAGE COMPANY, OR ORDER ONE FROM A RESTORATION SUPPLY CATALOG.

GAZING BALLS WERE THE HEIGHT OF FASHION DURING THE VICTORIAN ERA, AND HAVE BEGUN TO EXPERIENCE SOMETHING OF A COMEBACK IN POPULARITY. IN SOME PARTS OF THE COUNTRY, THEY ARE REFERRED TO AS "WITCHES' BALLS" FOR THEIR REPUTED ABILITY TO FRIGHTEN WITCHES AWAY FROM YOUR YARD. THEIR PERFECT SPHERICAL SHAPE CAN MAKE THE SMALLEST GARDEN LOOK LIKE THE PONDEROSA.

"Quite frankly, his taste is in his mouth. Did you get a load of that little troll over there under the azaleas?"

Containers

Most nurseries and garden centers stock a wide variety of containers for plants. They range from the plainest plastic pot to terra-cotta or concrete containers with formal designs in bas-relief, to copies of the wooden boxes in which King Louis grew his orange trees at Versailles. The simplest clay or wooden containers are fine, but a considerable amount of personality can be added to any yard with a couple of the more ornamental containers.

Choose the largest containers your budget and space can handle. They hold a greater volume of soil (which means that it won't dry out so quickly and will therefore require fewer waterings), and they add an impressive quality to the plants they hold. A pair of large containers can be used to mark the entrance to a path, placed on either side of a wall fountain, flanking the steps leading to a deck or terrace, or on either side of the steps in a swimming pool. Used this way, containers and the plants they hold act as attractive "signposts," indicating important locations in your yard. Placed right next to a door or gate, a single, large container, planted with any type of flowering plant, makes for a pleasant note on which to come and go.

A simple yet glorious combination: a big clay pot filled with red geraniums.

Terra-Cotta Pots

In areas of the country with mild winters, terra-cotta, or clay, pots can be left outdoors year 'round without any fear of damage. Because terra-cotta is porous, the walls of the pots will always contain some amount of water. Where winters are severe, periods of alternate freezing and thawing will eventually take their toll, resulting in cracked and crumbling pots. If they are not too large or heavy, you can avoid this problem by moving the pots into your garage or basement for the winter. If you can't move them, paint the pots both inside and out with a liberal coating of water-sealant. By doing so, you'll extend the life of the pots considerably.

Window Boxes

Although they are more often associated with the front, "public" side of a house than the rear, windowboxes are so effective at dressing up a house, consider them for *every* window. Even in areas where spring and summer rains are frequent, windowboxes are notorious for demanding almost daily waterings. Most would agree, however, that the charm these containers provide is more than worth the care they demand.

CONTAINERS

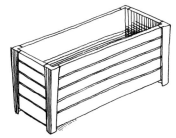

SIMPLE, LONG WOODEN CONTAINERS CAN BE USED TO DEMARCATE THE EDGE OF A PATIO OR TERRACE, OR IN PLACE OF A RAILING ON A DECK. THEY CAN BE FILLED WITH SOIL AND PLANTED, OR USED TO CONCEAL A ROW OF ALREADY BLOOMING PLANTS IN PLASTIC POTS, PURCHASED JUST THIS MORNING AT THE NURSERY.

WINDOW BOXES ARE ONE OF THE EASIEST WAYS TO ADD A LITTLE CHARM TO AN OTHERWISE PLAIN HOUSE. WATCH THEM CAREFULLY, HOWEVER, AS THEY NEED REGULAR WATERING AND FEEDING TO LOOK THEIR BEST.

THERE'S SOMETHING ABOUT THE SHAPE OF AN URN THAT DOESN'T EVEN REQUIRE PLANTING TO LOOK GOOD. BUT IF YOU CAN'T RESIST THE TEMPTATION, PLANT THEM WITH A CASCADING, FLOWERING PLANT.

TERRA-COTTA POTS WITH BAS-RELIEF DESIGNS ARE IMPORTED PRIMARILY FROM MEXICO AND ITALY. THE DISCREET DECORATION ADDS A NOTE OF SOPHISTICATION, JUST RIGHT FOR A FORMAL TERRACE OR ENTRYWAY.

THE CLASSIC CLAY POT HAS LOST NONE OF ITS APPEAL FROM ONE GENERATION TO THE NEXT. TRY GROUPING SEVERAL DIFFERENT SIZED POTS TOGETHER AND PLANTING THEM WITH A VARIETY OF FLOWERING PLANTS. IT WILL LOOK LIKE A HUGE BOUQUET.

HIGHLY ORNAMENTAL CONTAINERS CAN TAKE THE PLACE OF STATUARY. USED IN PAIRS TO MARK A STAIRWAY OR PATH, THEY MAKE A CLASSIC STATEMENT.

IF IT WAS *GOOD* ENOUGH FOR KING LOUIS, IT'S GOOD ENOUGH FOR ME. THESE ARE THE TYPE OF WOODEN PLANTERS THE FRENCH KING HAD HIS OUT-OF-SEASON ORANGES GROWN IN. NO WONDER THEY HAVE THAT STYLISH AIR TO THEM. BEST USED TO HIDE AN ORDINARY POT.

"Forget terra cotta. What about a hermetically sealed container for a few of these blessed fleas!"

Whimsy

There's something satisfying about adding little things to your yard not because you have to, but because you want to. Some can be purchased, some built, and others pulled together from items you happen to have on hand. Those illustrated on the facing page are taken from a random sampling of catalogs and garden shops.

The best whimsical items, however, are those that you put together yourself. They should be easy enough to build that they fall into the "weekend project" category. Whether it's an old-fashioned swing, a bird-feeding station, or a hose-guard with a hand-whittled wooden squirrel on top, these little things will help personalize your yard. The best thing about anything that falls into the whimsical category is that it can be approached in a spirit of lighthearted anticipation—an inspiring phenomenon if there ever was one.

It's been said that you can tell a great deal about a person simply by looking at the books in his or her library. The same could be said about the small idiosyncratic touches a person adds to the backyard: a smooth, perfectly arched branch used as a handle on a gate, the initials and date deftly carved into the back of a garden bench, a simple tin cup hanging from a crooked limb hook, right next to the faucet, perfect for big gulps of cold water on a hot day. These are gentle signs that someone has lived in and enjoyed this outdoor place.

And while there may be a sense of urgency when tackling larger projects—such as pouring a concrete patio or building a fence—one should take the luxury of lingering over the smaller ones.

A peep-hole for a dog may seem like whimsy to you, but to your dog, it's a social necessity. Just make sure that it's too small to crawl through.

The trip to the lumber store, lighting the light over your workbench, the careful measuring and cutting of wood, the smell of fresh sawdust and the pleasure of using the right tool for the job or having just the right-sized brass screw on hand. These are not things to rush over. There is as much satisfaction in the process as there is in the completed project.

If there are children in your household, instead of merely showing them the project in its finished state, by all means invite them to share in the experience of building it. Valuable lessons can be learned by quietly sitting on a stool and watching any creation, no matter how minor, come into being.

At some point, the time will come to identify a particular project just right for the formerly stool-bound student. Once they've gone from passive observation to active achievement, you'll not only have passed on an invaluable lesson or two, you just might have started a youngster on a lifetime involvement in a pleasurable hobby.

WHIMSY

HAVE YOU EVER CONSIDERED MOVING YOUR MATTRESS OUTDOORS FOR A LITTLE ADULT BACK-YARD CAMPING? WELL WHY NOT? IF BUGS ARE THE ONLY THING STOPPING YOU, RIG UP A MOSQUITO NET FROM AN OVERHANGING BRANCH. JUST THE PLACE FOR A LEISURELY SUNDAY NAP, TOO.

THE CLOSEST THING TO INSTANT NIRVANA: SETTLE INTO THAT HAMMOCK, AND LET THE BREEZE ROCK BOTH YOU AND A NEARBY SET OF WIND CHIMES IN A GENTLE RHYTHM. TWENTY MINUTES LATER, YOU'LL HAVE A WHOLE NEW ATTITUDE.

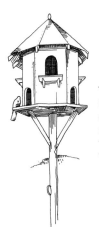

YEARS AGO, DOVECOTES WERE THE HOME FOR PIGEONS AND DOVES—BOTH AN IMPORTANT SOURCE OF FOOD AND A FUN, RECREATIONAL HOBBY. REGARD-LESS OF WHETHER OR NOT YOU ACTUALLY RAISE BIRDS TODAY, DOVECOTES MAKE A DISTINCTIVE ADDITION TO YOUR BACKYARD.

A LITTLE THATCHED BIRDHOUSE HAS A KIND OF POETIC CHARM TO IT, LIKE SOMETHING OUT OF A CHILDREN'S STORY.

HOW ABOUT ADDING A SUNDIAL AS A PERMANENT PART OF AN ENTRANCE OR GATEWAY. IT LOOKS RIGHT AT HOME IN A BACKYARD SETTING, GIVING ANY WALL THE LOOK OF THE OLD-COUNTRY.

HOW DO YOU KEEP TABLECLOTHS FROM BILLOWING IN THE BREEZE? WITH LITTLE HEAVY METAL CLIPS ATTACHED TO THE CORNERS OF THE CLOTH, THAT'S HOW.

"Just around the corner from 'whimsy' is 'crazy,' which is exactly where these fleas are driving me!"

It doesn't necessarily have to be a holiday for you to celebrate in your backyard. A pleasant, casual place to gather fosters celebrating the family on a regular basis.

BACKYARD CELEBRATIONS

One of the definitions Mr. Webster gives for the word "celebration" is as follows: "to observe a notable occasion with festivities." I like that. A "notable occasion" is general enough to encompass everything from a birthday, the last day of school, all types of traditional holidays, a promotion, the first ripe tomato, the tallest sunflower, not to mention solstices, equinoxes, full moons, or the first appearance of a special star in the evening sky. And the word "festivities?" That sounds like fun—pure and simple.

If you look at your backyard as an outdoor living space, it's probably the largest room you own. A typical backyard can gracefully accommodate a large number of adults for an outdoor sit-down dinner, a tribe of teens for a free-wheeling cook-out, or a bunch of kindergartners for that all-important birthday party. There's no need to worry about spills on the carpet, an errant splotch of catsup on the wall, nor the possibility of Aunt Hattie's heirloom spindleback chair winding up in splinters. And all that's needed for clean-up are a couple of large trash bags, a broom, and a hose.

Outdoor celebrations are by their very nature more casual than any festivity held indoors. With less constraint, people are free to let down a bit and have a good time. If I were Mr. Webster, I think I'd add that to the definition of celebration: *to have a good time.*

A Natural Place for Celebrating

A backyard is a small bit of the natural world, a window on the seasons. That many of today's religious holidays began

"As close as this flea is to my ear, celebrating is the furthest thing from my mind right now."

71

as an outpouring of secular respect for the natural world, makes the backyard an even more appropriate place to stage a celebration, in any way that might be meaningful to you.

The historical information in this chapter is not meant to suggest that we return to ancient ways of observing holidays. But when you look behind many of these old customs, what *is* relevant is our ancestors' connection with nature and their profound respect for the earth and what it produces.

That sentiment seems more timely today than ever before. If, in looking back, some of our present day celebrations are infused with a fresh breath of life, so much the better. A backyard celebration can be today's way of acknowledging the wonders of the natural world, inspiring respect for the environment, and having fun in the process.

Line a basket with plastic, fill with potting soil, and sprinkle with a little grass seed for a living Easter basket. Just the thing to observe the return of spring.

with the return of spring, the flooding of the Nile, and the growth of crops. During an early spring celebration in honor of Osiris, small clay likenesses of this deity were made and covered with grass seed. The celebration went on for several days, during which time the grass seed would sprout, a sure sign that the planting season had returned.

Osiris may be long gone, but just like hope, tender new blades of grass "spring eternal." If you're interested in continuing this fitting homage, it's easy to do with living Easter baskets. Simply line a basket with a plastic bag, fill it with potting soil, and sprinkle the surface with grass seed. Lightly press the seed into the soil, keep it moderately damp, and place it in a warm, sunny location. Within one week, you should have a nice stand of new green grass and the perfect complement to those pastel-colored Easter eggs.

Spring Things

For the past 6,000 years or so, ever since humans started to cultivate the land, people have held festivities to honor and celebrate the return of spring. It is a time of hope, joy, and great natural beauty. Easter, Passover, the Japanese Festival of Spring, the Hindu festival called Holi, the Chinese holiday known as Ch'ing Ming, and that ancient custom of May Day are just a few of the ways the world welcomes spring. Some celebrations are religious, others secular. All, however, have their roots in ancient ritual celebrating the rebirth of the land.

In ancient Egypt, the god Osiris was associated

An Outdoor Easter Egg Hunt

The best Easter egg hunts I have ever been invited to were held in backyards. Most of these events were attended by more adults than children, but once everyone was let loose to find the eggs, distinguishing the adults from the children was next to impossible. Easter egg hunts are like that.

There's no shortage of hiding places for the eggs in most backyards. And from a logical point of view, it somehow seems more conceivable that the Easter bunny might hide eggs in your yard, as opposed to under the sofa in the living room. And besides, who lets the Easter bunny in the house, anyway?

It was the Pennsylvania Germans who brought the tradition of colored eggs to America in the 1700s. The tradition took more than 100 years to catch on in the rest of the country, but catch on it did.

The Pennsylvania German settlers also brought with them the notion that it was the Easter hare who actually *laid* the eggs, a concept not as widely accepted as was the fact that the eggs were *colored*. Over time, somewhere along the American trail, the European hare was transformed into a rabbit and finally to a bunny. Although the thought of a bunny rabbit laying eggs might have to undergo a revision later in a child's life, it's a nice idea to have the children leave a few "nests" around the yard on Easter Eve. Make the nests from found material—twigs, grass, leaves, and the like—so this hard-working rabbit will feel right at home as it "lays" its multicolored eggs.

May Day

As popular as May Day has been throughout recorded history, it is rarely observed today. If you want to start your own May Day tradition, the field is wide open as to how you might want to celebrate it. Use the following historical information as a guide or a jumping-off point for your own May Day celebration.

May Day is, and always has been, a celebration observed by children. It is one of the world's oldest annual observances, with its beginnings in ancient Rome. Towards the end of April or in early May, the Romans held a celebration called Floralia, in honor of Flora, the goddess of flowering plants. Not surprisingly, flowers were the theme of the festival: Children wore wreaths of flowers in their hair, carried large bunches of flowers, and made long, flowery garlands. Once they arrived at Flora's temple, the garlands were wound around the columns as an offering.

The festival continued from one generation to the next, over hundreds and hundreds of years. It eventually found its way to England, where it took on added significance when, in the curious manner of all folklore, the day somehow became associated with the anniversary of the death of that legendary hero Robin Hood.

After midnight on May Day eve, village children all over England would traipse into the forest to gather flowering branches of the hawthorn tree (commonly called "may" tree

The Change of Seasons

The first step in developing any kind of a relationship with someone or something is simply to know and remember its name. To that end, here are the names of some important natural events that can be observed in your backyard. How you observe them— either in a private, silent acknowledgment, or a full-scale festival—is up to you.

The Vernal Equinox, on or about March 21, marks the beginning of spring. On this date, the sun crosses the equator, and day and night are exactly the same length.

The Summer Solstice, on or about June 21, is the longest day of the year and marks the beginning of summer. At this point in the sun's annual pattern, it is at its farthest point north.

The Autumnal Equinox, somewhere on or about September 23, marks the beginning of fall. The sun crosses the equator for the second time in the year, and day and night are once again exactly the same length.

The Winter Solstice occurs on or about December 21 and marks the shortest day of the year. It is the official first day of winter.

"I wondered what all those eggs were doing around the yard. Hardly a gourmet's delight."

73

MAKE A MAY BASKET

ON MAY DAY (MAY 1) MORNING, IT'S A PLEASANT SURPRISE TO OPEN YOUR FRONT DOOR AND FIND A BOUQUET OF FLOWERS. IN THE OLD DAYS, LEAVING FLOWERS ON A FRIEND'S DOOR WAS COMMON PRACTICE, MADE MORE INTRIGUING BECAUSE THERE WAS NEVER A NOTE OR NAME ATTACHED TO THE BOUQUET.

KNOWING THAT YOU HAVE A SECRET ADMIRER IS A GREAT WAY TO START THE DAY, EVEN IF IT HAPPENS ONLY ONCE A YEAR. IF YOU WANT TO CONTINUE THIS PRACTICE, HERE'S HOW TO MAKE A PAPER MAY BASKET, COMPLETE WITH A HANDLE FOR HANGING ON A DOORKNOB.

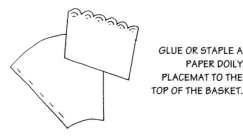

CUT A PIECE OF CONSTRUCTION PAPER (A LEFTOVER PIECE OF WALLPAPER IN A FLOWERED PATTERN IS A PRETTY SUBSTITUTE) IN THE SHAPE SHOWN HERE.

GLUE OR STAPLE A PAPER DOILY PLACEMAT TO THE TOP OF THE BASKET.

GLUE OR STAPLE THE SIDES OF THE BASKET TOGETHER TO FORM A CONE SHAPE.

STAPLE A RIBBON HANDLE IN PLACE AND FILL WITH A SPRING BOUQUET. DON'T GET CAUGHT WHEN YOU PLACE IT ON YOUR FRIEND'S DOOR—RING THE DOORBELL AND RUN.

in England). While in the woods, they would also look for a tall, straight tree to serve as a maypole for the next day's activities. Once found, it was cut down and stripped of all of its side branches, save for a little tuft of foliage at the very top. On the way home, the children would secretly leave small bunches of flowers at the doors of their friends, another practice that continues today with the tradition of "May baskets."

The maypole was paraded into town, carried on a cart decorated with flowers (it isn't hard to see the connection between this cart and today's parade floats), flanked by children bedecked in blossoms, cows with floral wreaths on their heads, a May Queen and King, and their "courts."

The May King, chosen from the village's population of chimney sweeps, was known as "Jack-in-the-Green." His costume consisted of a wooden framework completely covered with leaves. The highlight of the event was the dance around the maypole, with each participant holding the end of a streamer, resulting in an intricately woven pattern down the entire length of the maypole.

May Day contains one more, much smaller and private ritual, still practiced here and there in England and America. All of the young women of a village or town are instructed to rise at dawn, go out into the fields and forest, and wash their faces with the first dew of May. Legend has it that the dew keeps one beautiful throughout the year. In America, the legend has been modified somewhat: May Day's dew is said to remove freckles! If there's a young woman in your household, you might pass on the tip. As unfounded as it is in fact, it's still fun to carry on a centuries-old tradition.

Summer Hi-Jinks

Summer is "high season" in the backyard. For kids, the end of school is reason enough to have some fun. There are all manner of games to play, forts to build, nature to explore, and carnivals to stage. Then there are the traditional summer holidays of Father's Day, the Fourth of July, and Labor Day, and the not-so-traditional, like Midsummer's Night.

Summer is also the time for casual cookouts, sleeping outdoors, and making homemade ice cream. Any way you look at it, the backyard holds lots of possibilities for big summer fun. Midsummer's Night, at the height of summer, is a good place to start.

Midsummer's Night Madness

Like May Day, Midsummer's Night is one of the most under-celebrated "holidays" of the year. From one year to the next, it falls a day or two on either side of June 21st, and marks the longest day of the year, not to mention the official first day of summer. Now, if that's not something to celebrate, I don't know what is.

Over the years, we've celebrated this night in a variety of ways. Since there isn't any particular tradition to follow, at least in this country, our household has taken a fairly free-form approach to the festivities.

In Europe (especially in Scandinavia, where they have a special relationship with sunlight, considering how little they get during most of the year), Midsummer's Night is a time for general merry-making, with plenty to eat, music, and considerable quaffing. The real sight to behold comes around midnight when countless bonfires are lit on beaches and shorelines everywhere, tall flames reflecting across the water. Once darkness falls the scene takes on a fantastic, romantic quality. Not surprisingly, all this excitement traditionally results in a disproportionately large number of babies born the following March.

Even though I knew it wouldn't be put into service all that often, I decided a fire pit was a necessity in my own backyard. While I was at it, I made a wooden cover for the pit, which also serves as a nice, level, discreet stand for a birdbath. A couple of early fall backyard parties are warmed by a fire in the fire pit, but I really built it for Midsummer's Night and Halloween.

Most of us don't have access to the type of location that allows a rip-roaring bonfire, but even a small one contained in a backyard fire pit (see page 77) will do the trick when it's dark outside.

I'm not quite sure how it got started, but one year we rigged up ancient Roman-esque costumes for all the Midsummer's Night kids. The costumes couldn't have been simpler: an old white sheet, cut into a long rectangle with a hole in the middle. The kids slipped their heads through the hole, letting the sheet fall, front and back, like an old-fashioned "sandwich board." A short length of cord worked

The Best Peach Ice Cream Ever

The best peach ice cream, of course, requires that you have the best peaches of the season on hand. Don't bother making this when peaches are out of season; reserve fresh peach ice cream for special summer occasions and be content to dream about it throughout the rest of the year. Use fully ripe fruit. If you can find them, the soft-fleshed white peaches make an extraordinary confection.

*3 cups heavy cream
1-1/4 cups granulated sugar
1 cup peach nectar
1-1/2 cups fresh peaches,
  peeled and pureed
Pinch of salt*

Put cream in a heavy sauce pan and heat just to the boiling point. Immediately remove from heat and add half the sugar (a little less than 3/4 cup); stir until sugar is dissolved. Add peach nectar. Allow mixture to cool. Add remaining sugar to peach puree. If still not sweet enough, add additional sugar to taste. Combine fruit puree with cream and sugar mixture. Add salt and blend well. Freeze in a hand-cranked or electric ice cream freezer according to the manufacturer's directions. Best eaten as soon as the ice cream is thick and frozen. Besides, who can wait?

"I admit, that peach ice cream is not half bad—especially after it's soft enough to lick out of a bowl."

for a belt, and two pieces of string were used to gather the shoulders. Once the sheet was "bloused" around the belt, they were all suitably attired in what we dared to call *togas*. Well, they were, kind of…

The lawn had been ringed with Chinese lanterns earlier in the day. As soon as it was dark enough, we decided that the toga'd kids should be the ones to light the lanterns on this, the most auspicious light-filled day of the year. We asked them to line up and walk once around the perimeter of the lawn, and then instructed them to light the lanterns.

That task accomplished and dutifully admired, each child was given two sparklers (left over from last year's Fourth of July celebration), which a group of adults lit for them, all at the same time. We piped in some wispy music, and let them all do their best imitation of one of Isadora Duncan's numbers across the lawn, sparklers waving rhythmically in the lantern-lit dusk. As you well know, sparklers don't last very long, but that fleeting, dancing image will definitely last forever.

After the lantern-lighting ceremony and the sparkler dance were over, the mini-bonfire was lit and the obligatory marshmallows roasted. Everyone admired the Maxfield-Parrish-inky-blue night sky, just beginning to sparkle with stars. Although the ritual had no historical meaning, it didn't matter. Since then I have come to the conclusion that there are times when ritual has its own meaning, and beauty can exist just because it does.

By the time the good-nights had been said, everyone truly felt as if summer had arrived: a *real*

Homemade, hand-cranked ice cream— especially peach or strawberry—is one of summer's greatest pleasures.

summer, one sure to be filled with its rightful share of mysteries and pleasures.

The Three-Day Summer Holidays

The three-day summer holidays—Memorial Day, Labor Day and, sometimes, the Fourth of July— really seem to get our ignitions going. But when most people hop in their cars and head for the hills, some folks prefer to sit on their porches and wave good-bye. The neighborhood becomes blissfully quiet, there are few people in the stores or on the streets, and right over there, in the shade of the sycamore tree, the hammock sultrily beckons. Three days of peace and quiet in your own backyard retreat. Now that's a holiday!

This is definitely the time to invite over any friends and family members still in town, asking each to bring something good to eat. A big, mix-'em-up potluck, around the biggest possible picnic table, are what these lazy days are all about. And if someone doesn't make some fresh peach ice cream and a blueberry pie, when, exactly, are they going to make them? If you don't have one yourself, ask someone to bring a hand-cranked ice cream freezer. It's one way kids can learn to appreciate the truly fine things in life.

Take a look at the next chapter, Backyard Games, for a few ideas for some group fun before, during or after your potluck. Backyard Olympics has become a traditional Fourth of July event around our house, usually followed by a hellacious water balloon fight. It may not be as exotic as a trip to the mountains or the shore, but be it ever so humble, it's close-at-hand and everyone seems to have their share of fun.

Fall Into Your Backyard

Labor Day may signify the end of summer for most folks, but for one of my friends, it was the date of her annual Sunflower Lottery Party. Here's how it went:

Sometime in May or June (usually around Memorial Day) my friend would send out invitations for a party in her backyard, to be held on the Saturday of Labor Day weekend. Now that may seem a bit over-anxious, but because the party revolved around a 'Mammoth Russian' sunflower, the three-month lead time was necessary. The invitation read something like this:

"You are cordially invited to a Labor Day Party, to take place in my backyard on August 30. If you care to join in, the highlight of the event will be the measuring of "Sunny" the sunflower, at precisely 7:00 o'clock in the evening. Sunny was planted on May 1st in a sunny spot in my garden, in well-prepared soil. Within a week, Sunny had germinated, and on May 15th, had grown to a height of 3 inches. At this writing, on May 27th, Sunny is 16 inches tall. Sunny will receive twice monthly applications of a weak fertilizer solution for the remainder of the summer. If you care to guess what height Sunny will have reached by August 30th, send your guess to me (in inches, please) in the enclosed envelope. Each entry should be accompanied with $5.00 to go into the pot. The person with the most accurate guess takes all. You need not be present to win. Have a great summer. Hope to see you in August."

I recall this party with great clarity because a friend and I entered the "sunflower lottery." At 12 years old, it was necessary to team up, you see, because neither of us had a total of $5.00 for the entry fee. Having grown sunflowers before, we came up with our best guesstimate of nine-feet, eight inches (or 116 inches, as the invitation instructed us to write).

On the night of the party, at precisely 7:00, with some 30 or so guests gathered around, my friend and I discovered that even though we had missed the mark by a couple of inches, ours was definitely the closest guess. With a considerable pot of cash in our hands, we not only felt like horticultural wizards, but we felt rich!

This party certainly had its high quotient of silliness, but

BACKYARD FIRE PITS

SEVERAL MANUFACTURERS ARE NOW MAKING OUTDOOR FIRE PITS, MOST OF WHICH DOUBLE AS CHARCOAL GRILLS. GIVEN THEIR PORTABILITY, THEY'RE IDEAL FOR BACKYARD USE, ANYWHERE YOU MIGHT WANT TO TAKE ADVANTAGE OF AN OPEN FIRE'S WARMTH AND APPEAL. ALWAYS PLAY IT SAFE, HOWEVER, AND KEEP A HOSE NEARBY AND WATCH FOR FLYING SPARKS.

YOU CAN EASILY RE-CREATE THE LOOK OF A TRADITIONAL CAMPFIRE WITH A RING OF LARGE STONES SURROUNDING A BED OF SAND OR GRAVEL. PULL UP A FEW LOG "STOOLS" AND DUST OFF THOSE OLD CAMPFIRE STORIES AND SONGS. THERE'S SOMETHING FUNDAMENTALLY SATISFYING ABOUT CAMPFIRE ACTIVITIES—NO MATTER HOW OLD OR HACKNEYED THEY MAY BE.

"Are you kidding? I love fall. That's when I finally get the backyard all to myself again."

77

that's perfectly acceptable when you're in your own back-yard. In fact, it's what backyard living is all about.

Foolish and Fall-ish

Yellow school buses suddenly appear at one corner or another, part of their annual migration back to your neighborhood. A warm afternoon wind brings with it the sound of football and band practice. On your way to retrieve the morning newspaper, you notice that the lawn, a lacy spider web, and the newspaper itself are covered with dew. Fall is, as they say, "in the air."

The official first day of fall, on or about September 23rd, marks the autumnal equinox, a point in the year when day and night are exactly the same length. But by then, most of us—no matter where we live—will have responded to the change of the seasons. Fall is as much a state of mind as it is a celestial and earthly reality.

The pace of our daily lives seems to quicken. Like the squirrels in their near panic to hide every nut in the neighborhood, we humans respond to some signal in our unconscious to get back down to "business"—usually indoors. This is unfortunate. Across the country, fall contains some of the best days of the year to be outdoors in your backyard

Your plants, which may have panted and gasped during the heat of August, can breathe a sigh of relief now that the hottest, longest days of the year have passed. Annuals are suddenly revived into a final burst of flowery glory before declining for the year. Many perennials may decide, rather capriciously, to put on one last display of blossoms. Add a little early fall leaf color, and your backyard may look better now than at any other time of the year.

And then there's the fact that most of the insect pests will have disappeared, having completed their life cycle earlier in the summer, giving both plants and people a respite from their attacks.

Cooler weather, no bugs, and beautiful color in the garden—all the ingredients for a terrific outdoor party. Instead of going indoors just now, why not linger outdoors just a little longer?

No matter where you live, fall is harvest time. A great excuse for a fall party is to stage a vegetarian extravaganza—the backyard equivalent of cleaning out the refrigerator and serving a banquet of leftovers. The vegetable garden may

SEPTEMBER'S FULL MOON IS APTLY NAMED THE "HARVEST MOON." WHY NOT HAVE A HARVEST DINNER—SERVED OUTDOORS—ON THE NIGHT OF THE HARVEST MOON?

look a little tattered this late in the year, but there are still plenty of treasures to be found: the most luscious tomatoes of the season, little firm heads of broccoli sprouting from the sides of old stalks, and if a lettuce plant or two went to seed, there will be baby lettuces, planted by the wind, thriving in the cooler, shorter days of fall.

Sometime in September, ask all the friends you know who have a vegetable garden to cook up whatever's still clinging to the vine and bring it to your place for an outdoor vegetable pot luck. A few years back, we did a variation on this, limiting the evening's vegetable selection to "Tomatoes only, please." From a first course of cold, fresh tomato bisque, right on through to the green tomato pie (served, if you can believe it, with red tomato sorbet!), it was a delicious, entertaining way to use up a bumper crop of Burpee's Big Boys.

Fall is also the time to scour your yard, garden, and neighborhood for those found objects that make great seasonal decorations for indoor celebrations. If you grew corn this year, save the stalks in some dry location for use at Halloween. On walks, keep your eyes down (at least part of the time), and look for pine cones, great for all manner of winter holiday decorations—pine cone wreaths, tree ornaments, or even for use as place-card holders for a special dinner.

Unusual dried flowers, such as those huge hydrangeas, the plumed seed heads from ornamental grasses, or the grand flowers of the common Joe Pye weed or the yucca plant, are ideal for use in arrangements, just as they are, or sprayed a metallic color for a brazen New Year's Eve centerpiece. As you stroll around the backyard, pick up any brightly colored fall leaves that catch your eye. Scatter them across the tablecloth for a timely, if ephemeral, table dressing. For a more lasting display of fall foliage color, pin leaves to a foam or straw wreath form (available at craft and variety stores). This compelling emblem of the season is just the thing for hanging on your front door. If you spray the wreath with an anti-transpirant (ask at your nursery or garden center for this product), the colors will hold for up to one month.

Halloween

There's no better way to wind up a Halloween party than around a bonfire. As our daily lives become increasingly

Moon Monikers

The Native Americans had a profound respect for the natural world, and named each of the year's fourteen full moons. Although some had more than one name, the following have found popular appeal.

January	*Wolf Moon*
February	*Hungry Moon*
March	*Worm Moon*
April	*Planter's Moon*
May	*Flower Moon*
June	*Lover's Moon*
July	*Moon of Blood*
August	*Corn Moon and Sturgeon Moon*
September	*Harvest Moon*
October	*Hunter's Moon*
November	*Beaver Moon*
December	*Cold Moon and Long Night Moon*

In addition to their given names, any second full moon in the same month is known as a Blue Moon, which gave rise to the old saying, "once in a blue moon," meaning something that didn't occur very often.

"If it's time for the harvest moon, the first frost can't be far behind. And after that, no more fleas!"

abstract, commercialized, and separated from the natural world, there is something wonderful about coming face-to-face with anything *real*. Fire is real: From one generation to the next, for countless centuries, it has retained its power to hold humans in its primal magic, casting a spell on all those within its glow.

Of course, fire is dangerous (which is part of its attraction), especially when costumes and masks are involved. If you have a bonfire, no matter how small, play it safe by having a garden hose nearby and—if it's a children's party—plenty of watchful adults to protect the kids from their sometimes careless enthusiasm.

Having been present at many of these Halloween bonfire events, I can attest to the enchantment that a bonfire adds to Halloween night. It's gratifying to see the looks on the faces of all those junior ghosts and goblins as they gather around the amber light of the fire. It makes you realize that mystery and magic are still present in our modern world, just waiting to be called into being.

Even a small backyard bonfire weaves a spell of mystery and magic—the perfect finale to any Halloween party.

Thanksgiving

Although the idea may initially strike you as outrageous, why not hold your Thanksgiving dinner outdoors? Around the picnic table or perhaps on a blanket spread out on the lawn in your backyard? If you're fortunate enough to live in an area with a mild climate, or if Thanksgiving day dawns unseasonably sunny and warm, holding this feast outdoors offers a refreshing break in family tradition, along with the possibility of some real fun.

Your relatives may think you've gone around the bend, but there are sound reasons—both historical and personal—for vacating the dining room. Consider the following: Outdoors, after all, is exactly where the original Thanksgiving was celebrated in 1621—and Plymouth, Massachusetts, isn't exactly in the banana belt, you know. Any complaints about breaking with tradition can easily be fielded when you tell the complainer, "*Au contraire,* we are, in fact, continuing a great tradition started by none other than the first governor of Plymouth, William Bradford." That ought to keep them quiet.

And although historians place that first Thanksgiving celebration somewhere between mid-September and late October, which may have included the balmy days of Indian Summer, what with our changing weather patterns, who knows what this November will bring Any outdoor feast is, by its very nature, more relaxed than its indoor counterpart. This point could not have been lost on Governor Bradford. His guest list included some 35 staunch Pilgrims, 66 "strangers," one Indian Chief, and 90 of his braves. Not what you'd call a homogeneous lot. And yet that first Thanksgiving was so successful and free of rancor it lasted for three days!

You may not want your Thanksgiving celebration to go on for three days, but just think what the ameliorating influence of the great outdoors could do for your own collection of guests. Take for instance the way your brother-in-law holds his mouth when he chews his food, or how your cousin always remarks on your lack of matching salad forks, or the way your nephews are allowed to run wild through the house before, during, and after the meal. All of these petty, irksome incidents simply cease to matter when your Thanksgiving feast takes place in the fresh air.

Not only did Bradford hold the celebration outdoors, but he and his guest of honor, Massasoit, chief of the Wampanoags, presided over a great deal of activity during the meal. Activity may be too mild a word; to quote from *Celebrations: The Complete Book of American Holidays* (written by Robert Myers, published by Doubleday in 1972):

"Captain Miles Standish paraded his group of soldiers in a series of maneuvers…Blank volleys were fired and bugles sounded. Stool ball, a kind of croquet game, was played. [Chief] Massasoit…came with ninety braves who competed against the settlers in racing and jumping games. The Indians showed their bow and arrow marksmanship, and the white men exhibited their skill with firearms. The celebrants are even reputed to have played games of chance." Makes those nephews look tame by comparison, doesn't it?

If there are a number of children attending, consider setting up the croquet set and tell them about Governor Bradford and "stool ball." Most kids (and a fair percentage of adults) can sit and behave for only so long. Providing an organized release for some of that energy can take the strain off those who prefer their meals on the quiet side. It's probably advisable, however, to keep the muskets, bugles, and bows and arrows locked up.

To be fair, the Pilgrims' original three-day celebration was not a solemn, religious Thanksgiving, but the continuation of an ancient secular festival known as Harvest Home, well-known to the Pilgrims from their former homeland. Traditionally celebrated after the main crop had been harvested, Harvest Home was, according to one historian, an annual event characterized by "cakes and ale and hang the cost." Harvest Home festivals became so rowdy that none other than Henry VIII (a ruler not known for his aversion to a good time) let it be known that if the farmers were going to party with such earnestness, they should at least wait until the entire crop had been safely stored away.

Why, with all their piety and aversion to celebrations in general, the Pilgrims chose to celebrate their first successful harvest with a raucous, secular celebration instead of a solemn, religious one, is something we will never know. It wasn't until 1623, two years later, that the fall harvest was observed by sacred days of fasting and formal Thanksgiving.

Pandora's Turkey

Pandora's Turkey is the name I've given to the simplest and best way I know to cook a turkey for Thanksgiving, or any other time of the year. You'll need a covered kettle grill for this procedure. It's called Pandora's turkey because once the turkey goes on the grill and the cover is put in place, there's no peeking allowed— period! The best part is that you can cook a 16- to 22-pound turkey in 2-1/2 to 3 hours. Here's how:

1) Ignite five pounds of charcoal briquettes in a covered kettle grill.

2) Wash and dry an 18- to 22-pound turkey.

3) Stuff neck and body cavity with a few handfuls of chopped celery and onions, mixed with a few tablespoons melted butter and poultry seasoning. Rub outside of bird with vegetable oil or melted butter. Sprinkle with seasoned salt and pepper. Place turkey in disposable aluminum roasting pan.

4) When hot, arrange coals in even amounts on opposite sides of the fire grate. Put cooking grill in place, and position turkey (in its pan) directly in the middle. Put lid on the grill. Leave both top and bottom vents fully open.

5) Do not remove the lid until the fire goes out, approximately 2-1/2 to 3 hours later, at which time your turkey will be perfectly cooked.

"Soon as I'm done here, I'll take some of that turkey, but skip the yams and cranberry if you wouldn't mind."

SNOWY PASTIMES

ANYONE HAVE A BAD CASE OF CABIN FEVER? BUNDLE UP THE WORST OFFENDERS AND LEAD THEM TO A CLEARING THAT'S JUST RIGHT FOR THE CONSTRUCTION OF A COUPLE OF SNOW FORTS. LAY IN AN AMPLE SUPPLY OF SNOW BALLS, AND LET THEM FLY. THIS FROZEN VERSION OF A WATER-BALLOON FIGHT COULD GO ON FOR HOURS, AND IS JUST THE ANTIDOTE FOR RELIEVING THE WORST SYMPTOMS OF INDOOR-ITIS.

IF WINTER IS COLD AND SNOWY WHERE YOU LIVE, IT DOESN'T NECESSARILY MEAN THAT YOU HAVE TO STAY INSIDE. HAVE YOU EVER THOUGHT ABOUT BUILDING AN IGLOO? IT MAKES FOR A GOOD EXCUSE TO SPEND THE DAY OUTDOORS. AND IF YOU'RE A SUCCESSFUL ICY ARCHITECT, YOU'LL BE THE TALK OF THE NEIGHBORHOOD.

If today an outdoor feast seems to be more Harvest Home than traditional Thanksgiving, at least it's an historically accurate option. Contrary to artists' renditions of that first harvest celebration, the Pilgrims and the Indians did not sit at long tables together. There weren't enough tables in Plymouth to seat a tenth of the guest list. No, most sat on the ground, ate with their hands or took tidbits speared from the tip of a knife (forks didn't make it onto the scene until almost 100 years later), or ate directly from large community kettles.

Whether turkey was actually served at the first Thanksgiving is not known for sure. The colonists of the period were not big meat-eaters, which is not to say they weren't big eaters. A twenty-hour workday was not unusual during the harvest, a fact that contributed to the average pilgrim's astounding daily caloric intake of 6,000 calories! Typically, their daily diet consisted of a pound of corn meal or peas cooked into a porridge, pudding or bread, a pound of butter and cheese, and perhaps a mere 1/4-pound of dried meat, washed down with a gallon of strong, dark ale.

So, weather permitting, pull out the picnic table, set up the croquet set, and pass the ale. An outdoor Thanksgiving may be so successful that everyone will want you to host it again next year. And who knows, you may even consent!

Winter Wonders

In most parts of the country, winter is a season spent indoors, one that has the effect of increasing the pleasure of returning out-of-doors, once spring finally makes its debut. People who move from areas with cold winters to a more temperate climate usually do so because they dread some of the grimmer winter realities: blizzards, snows (or perhaps more accurately, snow *shovels)*, and ice storms. The most frequently heard reflection from these "snowbirds," however, often goes something like, "It's great here, but I *do* miss the change of the seasons."

In temperate areas, backyard living goes on pretty much year-round. For some it sounds like heaven; others fear the monotony of too much "sameness." I have lived in both temperate and downright hostile winter climates, and know that each region has its charms. It's wrong to assume that just because it doesn't snow, residents in mild winter climates don't know it's winter. As human animals, something deep within us responds to the change of seasons, no matter how subtle those changes may be.

In parts of the country where it is in stark contrast to summer, winter provides some profound evidence of how quickly time passes. It can be a poignant experience to bundle up and take a walk around your backyard when most of it lies under a foot or so of snow. Could this possibly be the same spot where you sat under the maple tree, grateful for the cooling shade during that heat spell in July? Is that bare, ice-encrusted limb the same one that holds up the swing, where the young ones practically disappeared into the foliage with each successive push? Do you remember that Midsummer's Night party, when your backyard was bathed in the orange glow of lantern light, barefooted children danced across the lawn, and the fireflies responded in an electric flurry of phosphorescent green light? Could all of that have been just a short six months ago?

Those who spend as much time as possible outdoors, enjoying the gifts contained in each season, surely recognize what the poet e. e. cummings meant when he wrote, "kiss the joy as it flies."

Something Special for the Birds

Feeding birds during the winter is fascinating to observe, and those birds really appreciate your offerings. The most important thing to remember about winter bird-feeding is that once you start, don't stop. Birds are not quite as free as they have been made out to be: Most species are quite territorial, and once the food gives out in one territory, they may not have the option of foraging for food in another.

Sometime around the high winter holidays, pick out a special tree and decorate it with treats for your feathered friends. You may not receive a thank-you note for your efforts, but you'll be amply rewarded with a wonderful display of wildlife right outside your window.

"How about a little something special for me? A medium-size rawhide chew bone would be nice."

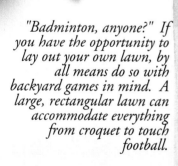

RULE 2. THE NET

"Badminton, anyone?" If you have the opportunity to lay out your own lawn, by all means do so with backyard games in mind. A large, rectangular lawn can accommodate everything from croquet to touch football.

BACKYARD GAMES

Backyard games come in all degrees of sophistication, from croquet and badminton to hide-and-seek and flashlight tag.

The best thing about any of these backyard games is also the worst—namely, a freewheeling disregard for the *official* rules and regulations. A fast-and-loose interpretation of the rules may make a game easier and livelier to play, but it can also cause problems when not everyone agrees with your interpretation.

Any organized game will be a lot more successful if played by *some* set of mutually agreed upon rules; they may not be the rules in the book, but there should be at least an agreement on what the "house rules" are, no matter how customized or idiosyncratic they may be. This is especially important when the players span several generations. An adult who insists on a certain set of rules, even when confronted with a child's objection of, *"But that's not the way we play it at camp..."* will suddenly be seen as something less than a team player. So start any game with a definitive statement of whatever rules you want to follow. Doing so will clear the path to a lot more fun.

If you agree that the main point of any backyard game is to have a good time, considerable leniency can be allowed in *all* aspects of game-playing. So what if your lawn is irregularly shaped and lumpy, or that you can't find one of the croquet balls and have to use a wiffle ball instead? The game of croquet will simply become that much more of a challenge and something to laugh over, rather than fret about.

"There's only one game worth playing, and that's Frisbee. Ask me. I know. I'm a dog."

BACKYARD OLYMPICS

HERE'S WHAT THE SEVEN BACKYARD OLYMPIC EVENTS LOOK LIKE:

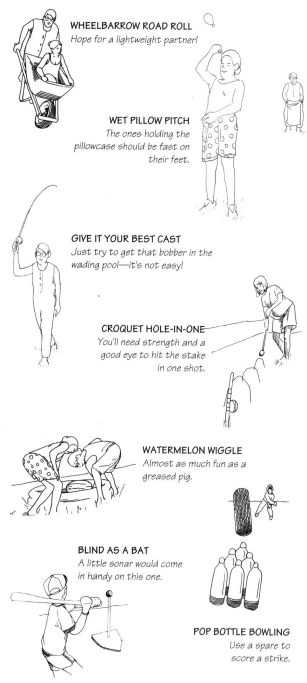

WHEELBARROW ROAD ROLL
Hope for a lightweight partner!

WET PILLOW PITCH
The ones holding the pillowcase should be fast on their feet.

GIVE IT YOUR BEST CAST
Just try to get that bobber in the wading pool—it's not easy!

CROQUET HOLE-IN-ONE
You'll need strength and a good eye to hit the stake in one shot.

WATERMELON WIGGLE
Almost as much fun as a greased pig.

BLIND AS A BAT
A little sonar would come in handy on this one.

POP BOTTLE BOWLING
Use a spare to score a strike.

Improvising backyard games and starting new traditions…that's exactly what the following suggestion for staging a "Backyard Olympics" is all about. It has become an annual event around here. We may drop a few events and add a couple of new ones, the names and faces of the participants might change, and new "world records" may be set (or invented), but the amount of fun the games produce seems to remain constant from year to year.

Backyard Olympics

Summer offers a number of opportunities for outdoor celebrations. Implicit in any backyard party is the potential for all to "do their own thing." Kids can jump and run and yell to their heart's content without much fear of parental interference, and adults can, if they are so inclined, act goofy without risking public humiliation. Why behave when you don't have to, right? With this thought in mind, I came up with the idea of staging a Backyard Olympics event to coincide with a Father's Day cookout.

High on the list of priorities was that the activity involve both kids and adults—together. And not wanting to spend a lot of time and money gathering equipment and supplies meant that using things on hand was important. Empty plastic pop bottles, old tires, garden hoses, a wheelbarrow, fishing pole, plastic baseball bat, and an odd assortment of balls were put into service.

Each of the teams comprised two people—one adult and one child. This left us with two extra adults, who graciously consented to act as official timer/referee and—just in case—medic. The medic may not have been called into action that day, but the referee had her hands full! The adults, it seemed, had a penchant for bending the rules, a fact loudly decried by the kids on opposing teams.

Here's how to begin the games: Mark two sets of identical numbers on small slips of paper and keep them separate. Put the first set into a hat and let the kids pick; repeat the process for the adults. Match up the numbers and you have your teams. *Note:* For the sake of harmony, we decided to avoid any parent/child teams. With a little quick and good-natured juggling, we successfully mixed up the teams.

There were seven stations in our original Backyard Olympics, all of which were set up on the lawn. Each station had preset objectives and rules (sort-of). The stations developed solely from the equipment and supplies we happened to have on hand. Feel free to modify the following any way you want.

Wheelbarrow Road Roll: Hope for a small teammate for this one! A twisting turning course is laid out on the lawn, demarcated by two garden hoses. Put your teammate in the wheelbarrow. Start the stopwatch and stay between the hoses. If you tip over, you have to go back to the start. Fastest time wins.

Wet Pillow Pitch: Water balloons and a pillowcase are all that's needed for this. Standing roughly 20 feet apart, one member of the team pitches the water balloons to his or her teammate, who tries to catch it in the pillowcase—without breaking! Made much more difficult by the fact that the balloon-thrower must toss the balloons backwards, over the shoulder. Three tries; most unbroken water balloons in the pillowcase wins.

Croquet Hole-in-One: Line up three wickets, approximately four feet apart. Plant a stake at the far end. The object is to hit the ball directly through the wickets and hit the stake in one fell stroke. Three tries: most direct hits wins.

Give It Your Best Cast: This one was tough, but we had a few "bobbers-in-one." Fill a wading pool with water. Outfit a casting rod with one of those red-and-white bobbers and a little weight. Standing approximately 20 feet away, try to land the bobber in the wading pool. Five tries (at least!). Most bobbers in the pool wins.

Watermelon Wiggle: Grease a watermelon (solid vegetable shortening works best). Put the melon in the wading pool filled with water. Using masking tape, mark an "X" on the lawn about five feet away from the wading pool. Place team members on opposite sides of the pool and instruct them to pick up the melon and place it on the "X." Only problem is, each team member can use only one hand! Three tries.

It Didn't Bother the Duke

If you think that improvising backyard games may be too untraditional for you, look at it this way: You could be starting a new tradition rather than breaking one. This is exactly what happened in 1522 when the Duke of Suffolk sawed off one of the ornamental wooden balls from a banister, in order to replace a ball that broke during a heated game of lawn bowls. The fact that the ball was slightly flat on one side, where it had been sawed from the banister, caused it to curve when thrown down the playing field. From that time on, lawn bowls has been played with balls that curve when thrown. Who knows what new traditions your improvisations may start?

"Having been to a few of those parties, the Duke's behavior doesn't surprise me a bit. The things I've seen!"

Blind-as-a-Bat: Set a plastic "wiffle" ball on a stand. Blindfold the batters and hand them a plastic bat. Now, the question is how far can you hit the ball? Or maybe, can you hit it at all? Five strikes and you're out!

Empty Bottle Bowling: Set up large, empty, plastic pop bottles as you would bowling pins. Position the player approximately 15 to 20 feet away. Then, instead of a ball, roll an empty tire down the "alley." Score as you would traditional bowling.

Just for the record, it took well over two hours for the teams to make it through all seven stations, so you might want to start your party a little earlier than usual.

Classic Lawn Games

Traditional lawn games include croquet, badminton, and bocce (sometimes spelled *boccie* and sometimes referred to as *boules*). Each has a long history, resulting in highly refined rules and regulations, including more or less standardized court sizes, especially for professional play.

As was stated in the introduction, backyard games tend towards leniency in the rules and regulations department. If the games are just for fun, treat the information that comes with the games as guidelines rather than the last word, and keep the accent on play rather than sport. If, however, you run with a crowd that takes winning seriously, be sure to keep the rule book close at hand. But once you see how complex and detailed they are, you'll completely understand why so many backyard sportsters make up their own rules!

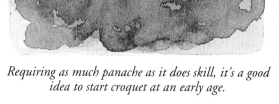

Requiring as much panache as it does skill, it's a good idea to start croquet at an early age.

Croquet

Unlike most other games, no one is exactly sure of the ancient origins of croquet. What *is* known, is that a game very similar to croquet, called *paillemaille,* was played during the 1300s in France. It made its way to Ireland, and from there to England where, interestingly, the London field where it was played is still known by the English version of *paillemaille*— namely, Pall Mall.

It wasn't until 1850 that the game became widely popular, when a London toymaker, John Jaques, manufactured a complete croquet set. Soon thereafter, Americans were introduced to croquet, and although over the last 100 years its popularity has waxed and waned, it has never completely fallen out of favor. What was once a highly refined game intended for the elite has now become a common, pleasant backyard pastime and one of the fastest-growing games in America.

Tournament croquet is played on a rectangular grass court, mowed to a height of only 1/4- to 1/2-inch. Keeping professional croquet courts in perfect condition requires the same meticulous attention as putting greens. Obviously, home croquet courts can be more relaxed and the court any size you want. If possible, the long sides of the rectangular court should be twice as long as the short side. And if a court 50 by 100 feet is not possible, 30 by 60 will do—a size most aficionados agree is as small as the court can be and still allow challenging play. If you don't have that much room, or if your lawn is of an irregular shape, decrease the number of wickets or set them up in any pattern you like.

Badminton

A game very much like badminton was played in ancient Greece and Egypt. Like all games that are fun to play, over many years it migrated to various parts of the world. By the 19th century, British army officers stationed in India took note of a game called *poona*, and took the game with them when they returned home. In 1873, poona was played on the grounds of the home of the Duke of Beaufort at Badminton, England. From that point on, the game was known as badminton.

Unique to the game of badminton is the shuttlecock, a half round piece of cork with feathers stuck in the flat end. Hit with the small, light racquet, the shuttlecock can travel straight through the air at speeds of more than 100 miles per hour and then suddenly slow down and drop to the ground. It is the curious behavior of shuttlecock that makes badminton such a challenging game to play.

Badminton is played in more than 70 countries worldwide. The International Badminton Federation oversees competitive matches. World cup games are held every three years and, interestingly, are restricted to amateur players. Practice enough in your backyard and you could find yourself participating in a world-class competition!

Official badminton games are played indoors, usually on a wooden floor. Most would agree that it is a much more pleasant game when played outdoors, on a grass court. The official size for a badminton court is 17 by 44 feet, a size easily accommodated by most backyard lawns. For a doubles game (two players per side), the width of the court is expanded to 20 feet. The badminton net divides the center of the court. An official net is 20 feet long by 30 inches wide. The top of the net should measure exactly 61 inches from the ground.

Badminton is similar to tennis in that only the server can score a point. The server hits the shuttlecock underhand; the serve must clear the net and fall within the boundaries of the court; failing to do so results in the serve alternating to the opposite player or team. A point is scored if the receiving side fails to return the shuttlecock over the net or returns the serve out of bounds. If the receiving side successfully returns the serve and the server fails to return the shuttlecock over the net, or hits it out of bounds, the serve is granted to the opposite side. Play continues until one side scores either 15 or 21 points (decided upon before play begins).

THE SHUTTLECOCK, UNIQUE IN THE WORLD OF SPORTS, WAS ORIGINALLY MADE FROM A PIECE OF CORK AND CHICKEN FEATHERS. IN 1909, SHUTTLECOCK MANUFACTURERS BEGAN TO USE FEATHERS FROM THE WINGS OF GEESE. THIS SOON PROVED TO BE IMPRACTICAL, HOWEVER, AS EACH GOOSE PRODUCED ONLY 16 FEATHERS THAT WERE OF A SUITABLE SIZE AND SHAPE. TODAY'S SHUTTLECOCKS ARE MADE FROM A VARIETY OF MATERIALS, INCLUDING PLASTIC AND NYLON.

"How was I to know that shuttlecock wasn't a chew toy? Those plastic feathers were awful!"

Bocce

Whether you call it bocce or boules, this is a great backyard game. The related game of lawn bowls requires a court larger than most backyards can accommodate, which is why most games of lawn bowls are played on public courts.

The rules for bocce are so simple that any age group can play, but enough strategy and finesse are involved to keep it interesting day after day. Indeed, in many parts of Europe, you'll find the same group of people playing on public lawn bowling courts every day of the week. Competition, needless to say, can become fierce.

Although bocce can be played on packed dirt or clay courts, grass makes for a more pleasant playing surface. Traditional courts are 12 by 60 feet long, although the measurements can be modified if the proportions are kept the same (such as 6 by 30 feet, or 8 by 45 feet). Whatever size court you make, just be sure that it is an unobstructed surface, with no trees, sprinkler heads, or other objects that would keep the balls from rolling in a straight line.

The perimeter of bocce courts are usually defined with a short embankment (at least the height of a bocce ball), sturdy enough to withstand being hit by a speeding ball. Long lengths of 2- x 6-inch lumber, well-anchored to the ground, will do nicely. Proficient bocce players use the side and back walls for banking and rebound shots.

Bocce is played with eight large balls and one smaller target (or object) ball called the pallino, cue ball, or jack. There are four balls to a side or team; they are made in two colors to distinguish the balls of one team from the those of the other.

Deceptively simple, long-time bocce players know just how fierce the competition can become.

A coin toss determines which team throws the pallino. The pallino is thrown by the member of the team who won the coin toss to determine the start of the game. After throwing the pallino (which must be thrown at least half the distance of the court), the same player throws the first ball. The opposing team then delivers their bocce balls until the point is taken or they have thrown all four of their balls. This "nearest ball" rule governs the sequence of thrown balls. The side whose ball is the closest to the pallino is called the "in" ball, and the opposing side the "out" ball. Whenever a team gets "in," it steps aside and allows the "out" team to bowl.

A team has the option of rolling, throwing, bouncing or banking its ball down the court, provided it does not go out-of-bounds or the player does not violate the foul markers. A player also has the option of "spocking" or hitting out any ball in play in trying to obtain a point or to decrease the opposing team's points.

At the end of each frame (when both sides have played their four balls), a designated official, under the scrutiny of the "captain" of each team, determines the points scored. The balls scoring points are those closer to the pallino than the closest ball of the opposing team. This can be determined either by viewing or by mechanical measurement. Aficionados always use rulers!

In the event that the two balls closest to the pallino belong to opposing teams and are tied, no points will be awarded, and the pallino returns to the team that delivered it. Only balls distinguishably closer to the pallino than any opponent's balls may be awarded points.

Other Backyard Games

Some games perfect for backyard playing don't require a lawn. The first two, horseshoes and marbles, can be played on packed dirt. Shuffleboard needs a smooth concrete surface for successful play. Volleyball can be played on almost any surface—sand, dirt, or asphalt—but is most comfortable when played on a lawn.

Horseshoes

The game of horseshoes dates back to a similar game played by soldiers in ancient Rome. When the Romans conquered the land now known as England, they took the game with them. From England, the game of horseshoes crossed the ocean to America with the early settlers and has been played in this country ever since.

The game was originally played with standard horseshoes (the type used to shod horses). Since the 1920s, special "open shoes" have replaced the standard horseshoe as the favored shoe for pitching; this is the type of horseshoe sold in horseshoe kits at sporting good stores. The National Horseshoe Pitchers Association defines an official horseshoe as follows: "A shoe shall not exceed 7-1/4 inches in width, 7-5/8 inches in length, and shall not weigh more than 2 pounds, 10 ounces. On a parallel line 3/4 of an inch from a straight edge touching the points of the open end of a shoe, the opening shall not exceed 3-1/2 inches. Where all measurements are specified as maximum, there is no minimum." That ought to clear up any confusion.

The object of the game is to pitch the horseshoes so they are caught by the stake—a feat known as a "ringer." In addition to ringers, horseshoes six inches or closer to the stake are counted in a player's score. The first person or team to reach 40 points wins the game. Tournament play usually requires the individual player or team to win the best two out of three, or the best three out of five games.

An official horseshoe court requires a space 6 by 50 feet. Although it seems like a large area, many suburban lots can accommodate a horseshoe court in a side yard—an underused space if there ever was one.

SINCE THE 1920S, THE SPECIAL "OPEN SHOE" HAS REPLACED THE STANDARD HORSESHOE AS THE FAVORED SHOE FOR PITCHING; THIS IS THE TYPE OF HORSESHOE SOLD IN HORSESHOE KITS AT SPORTING GOOD STORES.

"Horseshoes on a horse, and horseshoes off a horse, are two entirely different things, let me tell you!"

Marbles

For as long as there have been children, there has been a game called marbles. The object of the game is to knock an opponent's marbles out of a circle. In tournament play, the circle is ten feet in diameter.

The game begins by putting one or more marbles inside the circle (in official tournaments, 13 marbles are placed in the shape of a cross, inside the circle). The first player shoots his or her marble (called a "shooter") from outside the circle, attempting to knock one of the marbles inside the circle, out. When shooting, at least one knuckle must stay in contact with the ground. If players are successful at knocking a marble out, they are granted an additional turn, and can continue shooting as long as they knock a marble out of the circle.

If a shooter remains inside the circle after knocking a marble out, the player's free shot must be made from where the shooter rests. If, after shooting a marble outside the circle, the shooter also comes to rest outside the circle, the player can take a free shot from anywhere he or she likes, outside the circle.

Playing "for keeps" means all marbles knocked out of the circle belong to the person who shot them out; the term "for fair" means the winner is the person who knocks the most marbles outside the circle, but all marbles remain the property of the individual players.

Shuffleboard

Shuffleboard began as a type of street game played in England during the Middle Ages. It was known then as "shovel-board." Like most games, it went in and out of fashion (at one time during the 1600s it was relegated back to its humble beginnings and was primarily played in taverns), until someone got the idea to shorten the court (to 28 feet) and install it as a shipboard pastime in the late 1800s. By the early part of this century, a shuffleboard court became a standard feature on all ocean liners, seemingly ensuring the fashionable quality of this game for all time.

The first outdoor shuffleboard courts in this country were built in 1913 in Florida. By 1929, the National Shuffleboard Association had been created, and did much to popularize the game by standardizing its rules and holding national tournaments, the first of which was held in 1931.

In the United States, a standard shuffleboard court is 52 feet long by 6 feet wide. The most common surface for the court is smooth concrete, but shuffleboard can also be played on wood surfaces, provided they are smooth enough to allow the pucks to slide unimpeded from one end to another. The actual playing area of the shuffleboard court is only 39 feet long.

Shuffleboard can be played by two or four people. Each player or team propels metal pucks down the court using a long pole, with a special pushing device at the end, into which the pucks fit. This pole-like object is variously called a cue, a runner, a driver, or a glide. The object of the game is to score as many points as possible by landing your pucks on the scoring areas (triangular areas painted on the concrete); sections of the scoring area are marked with different scores: 10, 7, 8, and -10. Scores are tallied when each person or team has pushed their four pucks.

Play begins at the head of the court, with the pucks being pushed toward the foot of the court. When two teams of doubles play, a member from each team plays at opposite ends of the court.

Pushing a puck across the court so it lands in the scoring area is not all that easy. The game is made even more difficult by the fact that knocking an opponent's puck off the scoring area is permitted. Shuffleboard strategists not only try to keep their opponents from scoring, but try to position their own pucks in such a way as to protect those that have already landed in the scoring area. An "end" is completed after each side has shot its four pucks. How many ends are played, or what ultimate score constitutes winning, is decided upon before play. Common winning scores are 21, 50, 75, or 100. A match is the best out of three games.

Volleyball

Volleyball was invented in 1895 by William G. Morgan, the physical education director of the Young Men's Christian Association of Holyoke, Massachusetts. It was originally conceived of as an indoor game, designed for older members of society who found other outdoor sports too strenuous. Mr. Morgan called his new game "mintonette;" an onlooker of the game noted the volleying nature of the game, suggested the name "volleyball," and so it has been ever since.

Volleyball games can be played on almost any surface, but sand or grass is the best for cushioning falls—not uncommon in a spirited game. Tournament games are played with six players to a side.

The 30-foot-long, 3-foot-wide net is placed across the middle of a 59- by 29.5-foot court, the top of the net measuring 8 feet above the ground. As in tennis, only the serving team can score a point. The player at right back serves the ball; the served ball must clear the top of the net and stay within the boundaries of the opposite side of the court. If the opposing side does not successfully return the ball over the net, in a maximum number of three hits, the serving side scores a point. If the server fails to successfully serve the ball, play goes to the opposite side.

The first team to score 15 points is declared the winner; in the case of a 14 to 14 tie, the winner will be the first team to lead by two points.

Make It Easy to Play

Playing a backyard game is often a spur-of-the-moment activity. And nothing dampens a whim faster than having to go search for the equipment or finding the supplies so incomplete that it's impossible to play the game. To avoid this, keep all of your backyard game supplies in one, easily accessible spot. At the end of the season, round up all the boxes the equipment came in, try to find the instruction booklets, and check to see if you have a full set of croquet mallets, usable shuttlecocks, or a volleyball that still holds air. If there are missing pieces, now's the time to carefully search the backyard. It's amazing how a badminton racquet will mysteriously appear from behind the shrubbery and how missing croquet balls show up, inexplicably, in the treehouse. Comb the lawn carefully, because if there's one thing you never want to do, it's run over a horseshoe with a power lawnmower!

"That thing they play shuffleboard with looked enough like a Frisbee to me, but I may have lost a couple of incisors."

The most enjoyable outdoor "meal" may be the simplest: sitting on the stoop, in the morning sun, with that first cup of hot coffee. Makes it worth getting up a few minutes early.

Pictured above are the perfect outdoor accouterments: chipped crockery and inexpensive utensils. No sense worrying about breaking the family china when the goal of outdoor eating is relaxation and casual enjoyment.

ACS
1991

BACKYARD MEALS

ew human activities are governed more by habit than how, when, and where we eat our daily meals. No matter how many people there are in a household, meals are almost always served at the same time each day, around the same table, with each person laying claim to a specific chair in a specific spot, anxiously looking to make sure their favorite mug, plate, bowl or glass is right where it should be.

If you're going to get into a habit, make it a habit to eat in your backyard —at least some of the time. There's no need to make it a big deal; eating outdoors can be as simple as taking your bowl of cereal and cup of coffee out onto the back stoop, or eating a sandwich stretched out in the shade of a tree.

At first sign of a nice day, people in urban office buildings flock to any available spot to eat their lunches outdoors. They know how a change of scene, along with a little fresh air and sunlight, can make a difference in an otherwise hectic day. Even though the pace may not be as intense, the same holds true at home.

In a backyard setting, it's only natural that life's tempo slows down a bit. Your family or guests may sit back and notice the sound of the birds, the dance of the shadows across the table, or the colors of the setting sun. Because the environment is so pleasant, people don't seem to rush through their meal. They're willing to sit a little longer around the table, chatting, or simply enjoying the surroundings. And if you're a cook looking for compliments (and

"Tie on the nosebag, folks—anytime.
I'm ready when you are."

95

what cook isn't?), fresh air sharpens people's appetites, so anything you prepare is going to taste that much better.

People in other countries are far more likely to take a meal outdoors than we do in America. This has been true for a long time: In 1921, Ruth Dean, an important landscape architect, wrote "The plainest of meals becomes a bit of a feast, if it is spread under the grape arbor…with us Americans [however] eating in the garden is still somewhat of an occasion… true the breakfast porch is running into favor…but we still have to shake off the house entirely and get out from under roofs, for ordinary affairs. Probably the two chief deterrents are our national love of convenience, and our national insect!"

After some 70 years, our attitudes haven't changed that much. It is only on "occasions" that most of us think of eating outdoors, and lack of convenience and "our national insect," the mosquito, are still probably the two biggest deterrents.

During her many years of professional practice, Miss Dean had attractive outdoor eating areas built in practically every garden she designed—whether her clients requested one or not. No matter that her clients had never really thought about eating outdoors before. The fact that the place was *there*, close-at-hand and attractive was enough for it to be used extensively and with great enjoyment. Reflecting on this, Miss Dean said something simply happened to people when they ate "out among the lilacs," that didn't happen when they ate indoors.

It's not hard to understand the appeal of a table positioned under a leafy arbor—the perfect spot to while away a summer afternoon.

It would be nice if all of us had a Ruth Dean to lead us by the hand to an outdoor dining spot— already finished and furnished. But the fact is, creating a place for outdoor dining is a fairly simple and straightforward undertaking. All that's needed is a table and some chairs or benches, and a level, stable spot on which to place them. And while convenience to the kitchen is nice, attractive surroundings are every bit as important.

The place you choose for outdoor meals should feel comfortable and inviting. Keep in mind that our prehistoric ancestors took their meals in caves. As far as we may have advanced in the last 10,000 years or so, most of us prefer our meals in an environment where we feel some level of protection. Imagine the difference between eating a meal in the middle of a barren, one-acre lot, and the feeling of enclosure and protection offered by a small patio or terrace partially enclosed by a wall or fence, with an overhanging tree as a "roof," and large pots of plants to define the perimeter of the dining area and add a little color and interest.

The Comfort Factor

Once you find the place that suits you, a few permanent improvements will make the outdoor dining experience more enjoyable. As mentioned above, the only real requirement is a relatively hard, stable surface on which to place the dining table and chairs or benches.

The stable surface on which to place your table may be something as simple as a layer of pea gravel, spread over the ground, not more than two inches thick (any more than that and it becomes unstable for chairs and humans to stand on). Pea gravel is very inexpensive, and once you wheelbarrow and rake it into place, you're done. Spilled drinks disappear in an instant without leaving stains, leaves rake up easily, and the gravel has a pleasant "crunch" underfoot.

This somewhat rustic option is a favorite throughout the European countryside, where a pea gravel "patio" is often complemented by an arbor overhead, covered with a venerable grape vine. A weathered wooden table sits year 'round under the arbor, surrounded by mismatched kitchen chairs. It's a pleasant place where old folks sit and talk, sip their wine and maybe play a game of cards. The cook in the family is often enticed away from the kitchen heat to sit in the leafy, cool shade of the arbor to shell peas or string beans. It's a classic example of how the simplest improvements are often the best.

Beyond pea gravel, the next option for flooring, in terms of permanence, cost, and difficulty of installation, is a small "deck," constructed of a couple of runners and two-by-sixes nailed to the top. Built of weather-resistant cedar, redwood or impregnated wood, it will last many a season. Make sure you make it big enough for people to slide their chairs (or benches) back a few inches without falling off the edge.

More expensive, and probably requiring professional installation, are outdoor floors constructed of flagstone, brick or concrete. But perhaps that's for a later date, when eating out in the garden has become a matter of tradition rather than whim.

Our "National Insect"

To combat our "national insect"—the mosquito—try old-fashioned citronella candles. Used in great enough quantity to circle the table (six around a standard-sized picnic table), they work wonders. And instead of that electronic bug-zapper, put a strand or two of those mini-lights (the little clear ones so popular during Christmas) into the tree above your table. With such a plethora of attractions high above, you may well find that the bugs leave you

The Customer Is Always Right

Thomas Church (1902-1978), designed more than 2,000 gardens during his brilliant 47-year career as a landscape architect. Church was one of the first and most highly skilled proponents of using a garden as an outdoor living room. Much to his credit, he believed that one of the chief determinants of a design was the way a client actually lived—even if it resulted in a feature that he didn't particularly understand. What follows is his recollection of one client's unusual terrace:

"I considered mentioning that everyone likes to entertain on a solid terrace just outside the living room. But I remembered a flagstone terrace, recently installed, with herbs and alpines blooming between the stones. It's hard to walk on and impossible to furnish, but it is beautiful. Reducing glare, it brings controlled softness and color up to the living room glass. The main terrace is out in the garden under the shade of an oak. The family seems to enjoy it."

If you're hiring a professional designer to help you with the plan for your yard, make sure they remember, as Church did, that the customer is always right. Their job is to help develop your ideas.

"To think! They actually complain about mosquitoes. They ought to try fleas for a while."

97

entirely alone. Several manufacturers are making heavy-duty mini-lights available, sturdy enough to withstand year-round outdoor installation.

A more permanent, but very effective solution to the problem was developed by a friend of mine. Those who have spent much time in mosquito country know that these pesky insects are much more of a problem when there is no wind, than when a breeze is blowing. My friend capitalized on this observation by installing a ceiling fan over his family's outdoor dining table. A solid overhead roof is necessary to protect the electric fan from the elements, but if mosquitoes are a big problem where you live, it's a probability that summer rains are, as well. A solid roof overhead will allow you to eat in the middle of one of those wonderful midsummer downpours, and also permits the installation of a ceiling fan. All things considered, an ideal combination.

1) view
2) stool
3) light
4) table
5) protection from rain (if necessary)

The best seat in the "house" during the best part of the day is reserved for the outdoor cook.

The first requirement, view, will help immeasurably in producing a beneficial frame of mind. Don't place your grill where the only thing you see is the neighbor's untidy yard, a couple of air-conditioning units, or a storage shed. Walk around a bit before rolling your grill into position.

Once you find the perfect spot, outfit it with something to sit on, such as a stool or a bench, and a small, sturdy table for landing platters full of food. Set up some kind of a light so you can see what the food looks like when it's dark outside. (If worse comes to worse, equip yourself with a big flashlight.) Now you're set!

For the Outdoor Cook

Now that there's a place to sit and eat, what does the outdoor cook need? By all means, set up an attractive place to put the grill (if it's attractive enough, maybe you'll attract the cook out there a little more often). Nothing complements an outdoor dining room more than food that's been cooked over the coals!

As to the needs of the outdoor chef, here's a totally subjective list:

The Outdoor Cupboard

If it makes you nervous to use your plates, dishes, and glassware outdoors, leave them indoors. Invest in a set of dishes and glasses made of plastic, tin, or some other unbreakable material. A practical alternative to purchasing a special outdoor set of dishes is to set aside all the chipped or cracked crockery and designate them as your special outdoor set of "china." Keep all your outdoor supplies corralled in one location so you, or whoever might be helping you set the table, can easily find them.

Outdoor Food

Just as with dishes, the test for anything to do with food outdoors is, if it makes you nervous, leave it inside. The simpler the better: no *Beef Wellington* or *Salmon en Croute* allowed!

Outdoor food can be as satisfying as any in the world, but it must not be fussed over. Find the freshest, best ingredients you can, whether it's bread, fish, meat, vegetables or fruit, and let their natural flavors speak for themselves. Herbs—hopefully fresh from your own garden—are a natural accompaniment to outdoor foods, for any course, from soup to dessert.

The best trick for enjoying outdoor meals, especially when they are being served to a group, is to start preparing them early and serve everything either cold or at room temperature. Hot dogs and hamburgers, as easy as they are to prepare, must be prepared at the last minute and served hot off the grill—which is usually when appetites are at their maximum and patience at a minimum. On the other hand, grilled chicken, a thick steak cut into thin strips, or any skewered meat can be cooked well ahead of meal time and served whenever everyone's ready to eat. Look at it this way: If it's warm enough to eat outdoors, it's warm enough for cool food.

The recipes offered on the next two pages are guaranteed to take the heat off the cook. All of them can be prepared hours ahead of time. If, however, the interval between cooking the food and serving it is more than an hour, store the food in the refrigerator until about 30 minutes prior to the meal.

There are those who say—and count me in on this—that some food actually tastes better at room temperature than it does hot. The dishes that follow fall into this category. Use them individually, or combine them for a delicious al fresco buffet. And just think how relaxed you'll be when all the food is ready to go long before your guests arrive and the only thing left to do is enjoy your own party!

"What's this thing with garlic, anyway? I've got an important date later tonight."

COOL FOOD = COOL COOKS

GRILLED MARINATED FLANK STEAK

A FLANK STEAK TAKES ONLY MINUTES TO COOK OVER A MEDIUM-HOT FIRE. MARINATE IT FIRST, USING THE "ALL-PURPOSE MARINADE" RECIPE ON THE FACING PAGE, FOR 4 TO 6 HOURS OR OVERNIGHT. GRILL TO THE DESIRED DEGREE OF DONENESS, THEN SLICE INTO THIN STRIPS, HOLDING THE KNIFE AT A 45-DEGREE ANGLE. GREAT FOR OPEN-FACED "STEAK" SANDWICHES ON GRILLED FRENCH BREAD, FOR PUTTING IN PITA "POCKET" BREAD, OR FOR WRAPPING IN WARM TORTILLAS.

GRILLED CHICKEN WITH POTATO WEDGES AND WHOLE TOMATOES

MARINATE CHICKEN IN YOUR FAVORITE MARINADE FOR 4 TO 6 HOURS OR OVERNIGHT. IF YOU HAVE A COVERED GRILL, USE THE INDIRECT METHOD OF GRILLING, KEEPING THE CHICKEN AWAY FROM THE COALS. THIS IS THE SECRET TO GOLDEN BROWN, VERSUS CHARRED, CHICKEN. WHEN YOU PUT THE CHICKEN ON, POSITION OILED AND SALTED WEDGES OF UNCOOKED, UNPEELED POTATOES AROUND THE EDGES OF THE GRILL. WHEN YOU TURN THE CHICKEN, TURN THE POTATOES, GRADUALLY MOVING THEM DIRECTLY OVER THE FIRE. THESE DELICIOUS SPUDS ARE LIKE GIANT FRENCH FRIES. SLICE THE ENDS OFF TOMATOES, CORE, AND FILL CAVITY WITH OLIVE OIL, GARLIC, AND BASIL. GRILL AWAY FROM THE FIRE, FOR ABOUT 20 MINUTES.

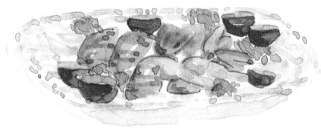

SKEWERED BEEF, LAMB, OR PORK

CHUNKS OF BEEF, LAMB, OR PORK MAKE IDEAL CANDIDATES FOR COOL FOOD. MARINATE 4 TO 6 HOURS OR OVERNIGHT IN THE "ALL-PURPOSE MARINADE" SHOWN AT RIGHT. THREAD ONTO SKEWERS, ALTERNATING PIECES OF BELL PEPPER, ONIONS, AND CHERRY OR PLUM TOMATOES. GRILL OVER A MEDIUM-HOT FIRE TO DESIRED DEGREE OF DONENESS. SERVE AT ROOM TEMPERATURE WITH A BIG PASTA OR RICE SALAD. GREAT PARTY FOOD.

GRILLED SHRIMP

MEDIUM- TO LARGE-SIZED SHRIMP COOK UP IN MINUTES ON THE GRILL. EXCELLENT WHEN SERVED COOL AT A STAND-UP PARTY AS A SUBSTANTIAL HORS D'OEUVRE. SERVE WITH PLENTY OF FRESH LEMON OR A SPICY DIPPING SAUCE.

GRILLED RATATOUILLE

ONE OF THE TRUE PLEASURES OF SUMMER, THIS MELANGE OF VEGETABLES ACTUALLY TASTES BETTER THE DAY AFTER IT HAS BEEN ASSEMBLED. PEEL AND CUT EGGPLANT INTO 1-1/2-INCH CHUNKS. COAT WITH OLIVE OIL, PLACE ON SKEWERS, AND GRILL UNTIL JUST TENDER. DO THE SAME TO ONIONS, BELL PEPPERS, AND CHERRY OR PLUM TOMATOES. AS EACH INGREDIENT HAS FINISHED COOKING, PLACE IN A LARGE BOWL. SEASON WITH A DOLLOP OF OLIVE OIL, SALT, AND FRESHLY GROUND PEPPER, AND AS MUCH CHOPPED GARLIC AND FRESH BASIL AS YOU WANT. MIX WELL. OUTSTANDING!

BRUSCHETTA

THICK SLICES OF CRUSTY FRENCH BREAD ARE ABSOLUTELY DELICIOUS WHEN TOASTED OVER THE COALS. CUT BREAD INTO ONE-INCH THICK SLICES, BRUSH LIGHTLY WITH OLIVE OIL, AND TOAST UNTIL NICELY BROWNED. IMMEDIATELY RUB WARM BREAD WITH A CUT CLOVE OF FRESH GARLIC, AND ADD A FEW SLIVERS OF GOOD-QUALITY PARMESAN CHEESE. A MEAL IN ITSELF.

All-Purpose Marinade

1/4 CUP VEGETABLE OR OLIVE OIL
1/4 CUP SOY SAUCE
1/2 CUP DRY SHERRY
2 CLOVES GARLIC, MINCED
1 SMALL ONION, MINCED
1½ TEASPOONS GROUND GINGER

MIX ALL INGREDIENTS TOGETHER.

"You can have that ratatouille, but send all the flank steak you want to in this direction—please!"

Kids and backyards go together. For kids, backyards are a combination of playground, experiment station, outdoor classroom, and, perhaps best of all, a "factory" that builds imaginations. Backyards are places that allow kids to reach for the mysteries of the natural world and for bringing its pleasures within their grasp.

BACKYARD KIDS

The conditions found in almost any backyard are fertile and protected enough to foster the best kind of growth in kids as well as plants. Given its position—both attached to the house, but separate from it as well—a backyard is a place where watchful adult eyes are felt but not necessarily seen, a fact that allows kids a unique kind of protected freedom. Backyards are also…

…A Place to Say *Yes*

If you have children in your household, or regularly play host to them in your backyard, the suitable role for a grown-up is one of a cheerful co-conspirator. All it requires is thinking like a kid for the moment, and saying *yes* far more often than *no*. In fact, instead of waiting to be asked whether it's okay to build a fort, have a carnival, or a backyard overnight camp-out, an adult can occasionally initiate these activities. At this point the adult goes from the role of a co-conspirator to actually being an *agent provocateur*—decidedly unconventional, but sure to raise your status in the eyes of the younger set.

It's no surprise that kids are remarkably inventive when left to their own devices. But as adults, we sometimes forget to allow a kid's natural inventiveness to run free.

For myself, one of the most adventurous trips I've ever experienced took place in a flower bed. It started when someone left a garden hose in the backyard bed of marigolds,

"Kids are okay. I just wish they wouldn't sit on me. Or try to put me into a costume for one of those plays."

103

adjusted to a slow trickle, in an effort to keep the plants from wilting during the heat of the day. Unnoticed by the grown-ups, who were much too tall to see such things, the thin trickle of water had carved a wonderful river canyon that wound its way around the thick and crenulated marigold stems.

To a much shorter person of a much younger age, this was not only obvious but fascinating. Crouched beside this miniaturized river, I was at once enthralled by the complexity of this marigold jungle. Best of all, of course, was the raging river itself, twisting around this bend and that. Incredibly intricate patterns of light and shadow changed with each breath of breeze. Unexpected and exotic insects walked on the marigold jungle floor and flitted through the marigold treetops that stretched toward the sky.

It didn't take long to discover that small long-boats, improvised from curled, dried leaves, could make the journey from one end of that treacherous river to the other, with me somehow firmly at the helm, guiding the leaf boat around dangerous shoals and demanding stretches of rapids. All up and down this flower bed river were signs that much less fortunate captains hadn't made it: half-rotted leaf boats caught on the mud banks, slowly decomposing in the warmth and humidity of the marigold jungle.

At some point I must have been called to lunch, or dinner, or I turned around only to notice a pair

To this day, the distinctive odor of marigolds brings back memories of that exciting flower bed journey.

of grown-up legs, and was brought up short. No matter. By that time I had memorized every turn and twist in the river, catalogued the jungle's insect fauna, and known the thrill of a successfully completed challenge, from one end of that river to the other, all alone at the helm of my long boat.

Many years later, in my own backyard, when my mother noticed me taking a too active role with my own child, showing her this and suggesting that, she passed on some sage advice: "Don't stand too close," she admonished. "Let your child have some time to herself. It helps develop the imagination." She was right.

The Right Stuff

By their very nature, most backyards are filled with all sorts of raw materials for play: trumpet vine flowers to put on the ends of all your fingers to magically become a witch, the seed pods of birch trees to crumple up and send showering down on unsuspecting friends as fairy dust. And give any four-year-old the garden hose (turned on to a trickle), set him down in a patch of dirt (soon to be mud), and he'll have the time of his life, for as long as you care to let him.

But as kids get older, say nine or ten, the "B" word—that would be "B" for boredom, as in *"I'm bored; there's nothing to do around here,"*—begins to rear its ugly head with increasing frequency.

Mud pies, marigold jungles, and trumpet vine fingernails no longer hold quite the fascination they once did. At this point, you'll have to take action and…

…Deal With the "B" Word

One effective way to deal with boredom is to designate a big box in your basement or garage as "The Box." Virtually anything can go into The Box: old sheets, pieces of rope, scattered parts of games, empty toilet paper rolls, old hats, shoes, gloves, leftovers from Halloween costumes, small pieces of lumber, you name it. Keep adding stuff to the box on a regular basis so there's always something different on hand. It may even eliminate those emergency trips to the variety store.

As for what to do with this assemblage of stuff, no instructions are needed. Once a child starts digging through that box, there's no telling what will develop. Just one last thing: Make it a rule that when they're done playing, building, or inventing, everything that came out of the box, goes back in the box, and the box is returned to its proper location. Well, at least it's worth a try…

After Dark

From behind the screen door a disembodied voice calls out across the porch, "All right kids, time to come in!" And from deep in the shadows, a half-block away, comes the inevitable response: "Aw, Dad! Do we *have* to?"

Playing outdoors after dark is one of the true joys of the warmer months: kickball in a pool of streetlight, the contained magic of fireflies in a Mason jar and, of course, getting the bottoms of your feet good-and-grass-stained as you run from one friend's house to another to see who's finished with dinner and finally free to come out and play.

Although it may sound like a kid's world, there's a little bit of a kid lurking within the hearts of most adults. As frisky as you may be feeling inside, however, the thought of an after-dinner game of flashlight tag may leave you weak in the knees. But don't let that stop you from instigating such behavior in kids.

Once the lights (and the television sets) go on, adults

Don't Tread on Me

It always seems that there's one backyard in the neighborhood that's more popular with the junior set than all the rest. If you're reading this book, then there's a good chance that in your neighborhood, it's your backyard. Having a popular hangout is a small price to pay for knowing where your kids are and what they're up to.

But there are days when a little peace and quiet is sorely needed. To that end, friends of ours developed a flag system to let the kids in the neighborhood know when it was okay to drop in, and more important, when it wasn't. They erected a flagpole in full sight of the street and bought two flags: an American flag and one from the Revolutionary War that displayed a rattlesnake about to strike, along with the motto, "Don't Tread on Me." When you're trying to make an important point, it doesn't pay to be subtle.

After installing the flagpole, the parents instructed the kids to look to see what flag was flying before barging into the backyard. When Old Glory was flying, everyone was welcome. If the rattlesnake flag was up, well, anyone over four years old could figure that one out. If you can't find the "Don't Tread on Me" flag locally, see pages 122-123 for mail-order sources.

"You know it's the oddest thing: Whenever the kids have to stop playing, I do too. Is that strange, or what?"

KIDSTUFF IN THE BACKYARD

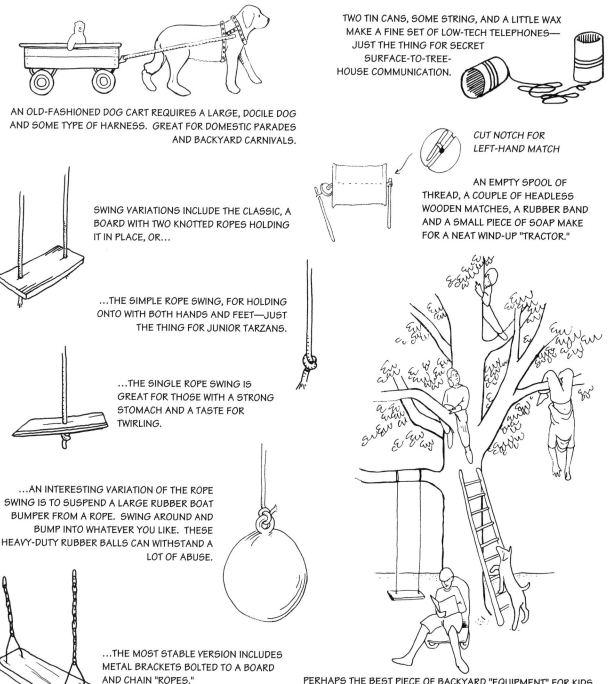

AN OLD-FASHIONED DOG CART REQUIRES A LARGE, DOCILE DOG AND SOME TYPE OF HARNESS. GREAT FOR DOMESTIC PARADES AND BACKYARD CARNIVALS.

TWO TIN CANS, SOME STRING, AND A LITTLE WAX MAKE A FINE SET OF LOW-TECH TELEPHONES— JUST THE THING FOR SECRET SURFACE-TO-TREE-HOUSE COMMUNICATION.

CUT NOTCH FOR LEFT-HAND MATCH

AN EMPTY SPOOL OF THREAD, A COUPLE OF HEADLESS WOODEN MATCHES, A RUBBER BAND AND A SMALL PIECE OF SOAP MAKE FOR A NEAT WIND-UP "TRACTOR."

SWING VARIATIONS INCLUDE THE CLASSIC, A BOARD WITH TWO KNOTTED ROPES HOLDING IT IN PLACE, OR…

…THE SIMPLE ROPE SWING, FOR HOLDING ONTO WITH BOTH HANDS AND FEET—JUST THE THING FOR JUNIOR TARZANS.

…THE SINGLE ROPE SWING IS GREAT FOR THOSE WITH A STRONG STOMACH AND A TASTE FOR TWIRLING.

…AN INTERESTING VARIATION OF THE ROPE SWING IS TO SUSPEND A LARGE RUBBER BOAT BUMPER FROM A ROPE. SWING AROUND AND BUMP INTO WHATEVER YOU LIKE. THESE HEAVY-DUTY RUBBER BALLS CAN WITHSTAND A LOT OF ABUSE.

…THE MOST STABLE VERSION INCLUDES METAL BRACKETS BOLTED TO A BOARD AND CHAIN "ROPES."

PERHAPS THE BEST PIECE OF BACKYARD "EQUIPMENT" FOR KIDS IS A BIG TREE. THERE'S NO END TO THE ADVENTURE AND ATTRACTION IT OFFERS.

tend to the notion that indoors is the place to be. But instead of calling them inside after dark, why not turn the tables and call the kids outdoors for a change. The instant kids receive such an invitation, they know something special is up. In case you've forgotten some of the slightly ridiculous, fun things that can be done outdoors after dark, here are some of the things you've been missing:

Flashlights are an all but indispensable tool. A trusty flashlight can be transformed into anything from a way of turning your face into a scary mask (by simply shining the light straight up from your chin) to a "laser" beam, to a means of telegraphing messages to your friend across the street or, even better, through the night sky to a distant planet!

Flashlight Hide-and-Seek

Even if there's only one flashlight that actually works in your house, that's enough for Flashlight Hide-and-Seek. The first order of business is to identify "home"—the trunk of a tree, a post, a picnic table or any other landmark will do. "It" is given the flashlight and, with eyes covered, counts to 100 standing next to home. The other players hide while "It" counts. When "It" announces "Ready or not, here I come!" the game begins.

The object is for the hidden players to make it back to home without being caught in the light of the flashlight. In order to be declared out of the game, "It" not only must catch a player in the beam of light, but must also call out the identity of the player. Flashlight hide-and-seek is actually a lot more fun than hide-and-seek played during daylight hours. Be prepared to play for a long time.

Backyard Theatrics

If your kids have a theatrical bent, why not try a nighttime play. Because advance planning is needed, suggest the idea early in the week and set a specific time and place, such as "Friday at 9 o'clock sharp in Jennie's backyard." This gives the kids a chance to work on the script and to round up costumes and props. The kids can even turn this into a money-making venture by printing up playbills and selling tickets and refreshments, with the proceeds being divided among the cast.

Nighttime Mysteries

There are so many fascinating things to see at night, it almost seems a shame that we no longer live outdoors year 'round. One night, after playing cards but before going to bed, a group of us went outside to smell the night air. Someone spied a shooting star, and then another. Before you knew it, we were all on our backs on the lawn, patient witnesses to a natural light show. Like an alarm, every time a star sailed across the sky, a chorus of ooohs and aaahhs sounded. Amazingly, we saw 27 shooting stars in 40 minutes. If we had gone to bed as we "should" have, we would have missed them all.

In addition to shooting stars, there are moths that appear only at night, plants, such as the moonflower and the night-blooming cereus, which blossom after dark, those much-maligned but relatively harmless night-flyers, bats, and in many parts of the country, the most mysterious and fascinating of all nocturnal insects, fireflies. If you have a pair of binoculars handy, and the night skies are clear, take a look at the full moon. Even a low-powered pair will reveal amazing sights, sure to impress both kids and adults. And if you're lucky, maybe you'll get a glimpse of that owl that lives in your neighborhood, as I once did, gliding silently through the night—a stunning sight if ever there was one.

If you agree that summer is a good time to relax the house rules a bit, let the kids stay up a little later than normal to do some nighttime exploring in the backyard. What they discover may stay with them for a lifetime.

"Flashlight or no flashlight, I've got to go to bed!"

NIGHTTIME SUPPLIES

HERE ARE SOME OF THE MUST-HAVES FOR HANGING OUT IN THE BACKYARD AT NIGHT:

JUST IN CASE SOMEONE ACCIDENTALLY LOCKS THE BACK DOOR, ATTACH A KEY TO A RUBBER BAND AND PUT IT AROUND YOUR WRIST. IT MAY COME IN HANDY IF NATURE CALLS IN THE MIDDLE OF THE NIGHT.

EACH CAMPER SHOULD HAVE HIS OR HER OWN FLASHLIGHT. THEY'RE GREAT MULTI-PURPOSE ACCESSORIES, USEFUL FOR FLASHLIGHT HIDE-AND-SEEK, READING IN THE DARK, FINDING THE WAY TO THE HOUSE, SENDING CODED MESSAGES ACROSS THE YARD, OR FOR TRYING TO ATTRACT THE ATTENTION OF LOW-FLYING UFOs.

IF THE CAMPERS ARE OLD ENOUGH AND KNOW HOW TO HANDLE A CAMP LANTERN, IT LENDS AN AUTHENTIC QUALITY TO THE CAMP-OUT AND PLENTY OF GOOD LIGHT.

DOGS LIKE TO GO CAMPING, TOO, AND MAKE GOOD TENT-MATES—NOT TO MENTION SUPERLATIVE DEFENDERS OF THE CAMPSITE.

DON'T FORGET A FEW LUXURY ITEMS, SUCH AS A GOOD BOOK WITH SCARY STORIES, SOMETHING TO SNACK ON IN THE WEE HOURS OF THE NIGHT, AND THAT FAVORITE STUFFED ANIMAL, FOR THOSE WHO WON'T LEAVE HOME WITHOUT IT.

Adults can help out not only by serving as the audience, but by rigging up a stage, complete with curtains—a task easily accomplished with a couple of long stakes, some clothesline, clothespins, and a couple of old sheets.

The cover of darkness heightens the drama and increases everyone's imagination, so don't over-light the "stage." Garden centers and hardware stores carry low-voltage outdoor lighting kits that can be arranged in any configuration you want, with the advantage of being able to be plugged into a standard electrical outlet. If you don't want to go to this expense, a few large, battery-powered lanterns will do, as will a camp lantern suspended over the stage area.

Backyard Camping

Much has been written about camping in our fabulous national parks, but what about suggesting to kids that they have a camp-out right in the backyard? If a tent is not available, construct one from those all-purpose supplies—clothesline, clothespins, a couple of long stakes and one or two old sheets. Spread a blanket on the floor of the tent, and put a couple of sleeping bags on top of it. Almost every kid will welcome a flashlight and assurances that the back door will remain unlocked and a light left on in the bathroom.

What's amazing is the way a backyard is transformed at night. After the good-nights have been said and the door to the house closed, the sounds of cars, birds (yes, there are birds that sing at night, especially if there's a full moon), sirens, the neighbor's television set or, if you're lucky, the hoot of an owl, are suddenly all the more pronounced. Before returning to your tent, lie on your back with your eyes open for a just a few minutes before slumbering off, and you'll be treated to the sight of a night sky brighter than you thought possible, thrown across a heaven more vast than anything imaginable. These are pleasant sights on which to dream. Or, wander around a moonlit yard when all the rest of the world is asleep, and find yourself in a world of your own, something like Puck's in Shakespeare's *A Midsummer Night's Dream.*

As familiar as your backyard may be during the day, take another look at it after dark. Combined with sufficient imagination and an urge to play, you just might find yourself in an exotic nightscape filled with enough adventure to delight us all.

Store-Bought Play Structures

There is an impressive array of play structures available today, some so complete they look like small villages. Swings, slides, monkey bars, and elevated forts with canvas roofs, are all connected in a single, well-designed and constructed unit. For the affluent or indulgent parent, these play structures are quite a temptation. The important question, however, is do kids like them?

Initially, you bet. What kid wouldn't? Their well-thought-out design, however, seems to contain an unfortunate static, lifeless quality, which increases over time. There's little room for a child's imagination to take over and customize the structure to suit their own needs. It's all been done for them and admittedly, done well. Once they figure out that there's a definite limit to the type of fun that can be had with one of these units, however, kids tend to abandon them for more interactive arenas.

If the truth were known, most sophisticated play structures represent an adult's view of what a child should want. From a child's point of view, the best of all possible play areas would be an abandoned lot with lots of tall grass, a few big trees with perilously precarious limbs, lots of leftover lumber and empty cardboard boxes, and full complement of tools to use (or mis-use) in gleeful abandon. Just the thought of such a place sends most parents into paroxysms of horror.

Somewhere between the manufactured perfection of store-bough play structures, and the wild and wooly allure of a vacant lot, lies a happy medium where both kids and adults will be content. It's been my experience that the simplest swing, an unadorned tree platform with a rickety rope ladder, and the old-fashioned sandbox—to name just a few—fit the bill quite nicely.

One-Act Plays

Most backyard theater directors agree that outdoor performances should be kept as simple as possible. One-act plays fit the bill exactly. They require only one stage set, usually a minimum number of actors, and they don't strain the patience of an audience that may include a number of junior theatergoers.

If a favorite one-act play doesn't come to mind, there are many anthologies available at your local library. Most will be grouped together by a theme, such as modern plays, famous plays, or the best American one-act plays. There are also collections of one-act plays specifically for young audiences.

One family I know invites two other families over to their place on a regular basis, each being charged with putting on a one-act play. Everyone has their turn on the stage and in the audience, and the evening's entertainment lasts no longer than one conventional three-act play. Cook up some popcorn and enjoy the show!

"Listen to me. I saw the rehearsals. It'll open and close in one night."

WILLOW
AND ALDER
FLYCATCHERS
L 4¾"

LEAST
FLYCATCHER
L 4½"

Zinnias make great landing pads for passing butterflies. This viceroy is one of the more interesting members of the butterfly clan. Its markings mimic those of the monarch butterfly, a species predators leave alone because of their disagreeable flavor. The viceroys don't share this trait, but none of their enemies can tell the difference between the two. If you become interested in wildlife, be sure to keep a pair of binoculars close at hand. It's a wild and interesting world out there.

ACS
1991

BACKYARD NATURALIST

In C. S. Lewis's classic children's book, *The Lion, the Witch and the Wardrobe*, the children enter a magical land by simply stepping through the doors of a wardrobe. And Alice did nothing more than fall down a rabbit hole and found herself in that famous Wonderland.

On close inspection, you'll find an equally magical world right outside your back door. Any backyard is a minute slice of the larger natural environment, filled with a sampling of nature's intrigues. And as in those fictional stories, gaining access to this "other world" is as easy as falling off your back porch.

All it takes to become a backyard naturalist is a curious mind, the desire to be out-of-doors, and a nearby library. Gerald Durrell, in his outstanding book, *A Practical Guide for the Amateur Naturalist*, writes "A naturalist is lucky in two respects. First, he enjoys every bit of the world about him and has a much more enriched life than someone who is not interested in nature. Second, he can indulge his hobby in any place at any time, for a naturalist will be fascinated to watch nature struggling to exist in the midst of a great city as well as observe its riotous splendor in a tropical forest. He can be equally interested and moved by the great herds on the African plains or by the earwigs in his backyard."

Those earwigs may not be of special interest to you, but they're certain to interest any child. Being lower to the ground and with their innate curiosity about the world, children make great amateur naturalists. They will pick up anything that catches their interest, from earthworms to

"So what do they think I am? Unnatural?"

SUPPLIES FOR THE NATURALIST

ONE OF THE MOST ENJOYABLE THINGS ABOUT FINDING A NEW ACTIVITY OR HOBBY IS ASSEMBLING A SET OF SUPPLIES. ILLUSTRATED HERE ARE A FEW INDISPENSABLES FOR THE AMATEUR NATURALIST.

SKETCHES ARE INVALUABLE FOR IDENTIFYING THOSE UNIDENTIFIABLE CREATURES.

A MAGNIFYING GLASS COMES IN HANDY WHEN YOU'RE HOT ON THE TRAIL OF A SUSPECT THAT HAS LEFT BEHIND NOTHING BUT MINUSCULE TRACKS. ALSO GREAT FOR INSPECTING SMALL INSECTS.

NOTHING LIKE AN EMPTY MAYONNAISE JAR WITH A PERFORATED COVER TO SERVE AS A TEMPORARY OBSERVATION TANK.

ALTHOUGH YOU MAY BECOME SO INTERESTED IN WHAT YOU'RE DOING THAT YOU FORGET ALL ABOUT FOOD, AT SOME POINT YOUR HUNGER PANGS WILL BRING YOU BACK TO REALITY. PACK A LUNCH TO GO.

NOT ALL BACKYARD WILDLIFE CAN BE VIEWED UP CLOSE. A PAIR OF BINOCULARS COMES IN HANDY FOR VIEWING THAT FLOCK OF CANADIAN GEESE THAT JUST MIGHT PASS OVERHEAD ON THEIR WAY SOUTH.

A POCKET KNIFE IS INDISPENSABLE FOR OUTDOOR EXPLORATIONS.

fallen acorns, wanting to know *what* it is and, of course, "*why?*" These questions often present a problem, as the resident adult may not know the answers, but that's what the library is for.

One Way to Get Started

One summer, a few weeks before school was to start, the 11-year-old regulars around our house were feeling the heavy hand of boredom. As an antidote, I asked them whether or not they were interested in becoming amateur naturalists. When they asked what a naturalist was, I admit I had to turn to the dictionary for the official definition, which, unfortunately, was so vague and unimaginative I made up my own. "A naturalist," I professed, "is like a sleuth—you know, a detective." "Do they ever get to solve murders?" one child asked. "Of course. The backyard is full of murder and mayhem. It is also full of miracles, unimaginable beauty and unsolved mysteries." I had definitely piqued their interest.

"Tomorrow," I suggested, "I want you to get started by going into the backyard for twenty minutes and write down every living thing you see, including anything that had once been living (this, in keeping with the murder mystery theme), and what it was doing during the period you observed it. If you don't know the name of something, draw a picture of it and we'll identify it later."

Of course they wanted to get started right away, but I thought I'd better take a backyard "reality check," just to make sure I wasn't sending them on a fruitless expedition, or about to be caught completely off-guard by the questions they might ask.

In My Own Backyard

As well as I know my own backyard, which is small and in an old urban neighborhood, it's amazing what looking at it from a different point of view will do.

It was dusk by the time I headed out the back door. One of our cats was ready for his evening stroll and decided to accompany me on my short nature hike. As I stood on the back porch, the first thing I noticed were the sounds of the birds, the crickets, and the cicadas. I found this reassuring, not only because there were such readily apparent signs of life, but also because I actually knew a little about the life habits of the creatures I was listening to.

The large sycamore tree that grows in our patio almost completely blocked my view of the sky, but the chip-chip-chipping sounds of the neighborhood tribe of chimney swifts filtered down. Every summer evening they careen and speed overhead, dipping and turning, all the while talking to each other with their party-like chatter. Chimney swifts eat on the run, so to speak, snatching insects right out of the air—and do they eat! They have to, in order to keep up their energy. Except during periods of heavy rain, chimney swifts fly continuously from dawn to dusk, never resting on the ground. A few minutes later I stood on the stone wall and watched as the swifts, hundreds of them, descended Mary Poppins-like, into the darkness of my neighbor's chimney, where they congregate every night. In the wild, chimney swifts spend the night hanging in hollowed-out trees and on the sides of caves and cliffs, even attaching their little nests to the vertical surfaces. I wondered whether or not they, like dairy cows, always lined up in the same order every evening, and dropped into the chimney in an orderly sequence. That question may be one of the "unsolved mysteries of nature" I told the kids about.

A group of grackles and blackbirds suddenly appeared on the brick wall at the rear of my yard. They took offense at the sight of Bruno, my feline companion, squawking insults in a very loud and derogatory manner. In a flattened ear, tail-twitching retreat, Bruno hightailed it under some low-branching shrubs. In this case, the cat—normally thought to be a predator of birds—was the one who was preyed upon, at least verbally.

I walked back to the porch to get a better look inside the top of a neighboring honeysuckle bush. There I saw an empty robin's nest, the inhabitants of which I had monitored every day earlier in the year. Three young robins made it through infancy and were coaxed into a life's flight of their own. The babies hatched out of those elegant pale blue eggs on Mother's Day. I remember because we were supposed to have a picnic, but a warm rain altered our plans. We had our lunch on the back porch instead, and were privileged with a small miracle of nature, right before our eyes, a perfect reminder of the holiday.

A FEW MINUTES LATER, I STOOD ON THE STONE WALL AND WATCHED AS THE SWIFTS—HUNDREDS OF THEM—DESCENDED MARY POPPINS-LIKE INTO THE DARKNESS OF MY NEIGHBOR'S CHIMNEY, WHERE THEY CONGREGATE EVERY NIGHT.

"Big Mr. Naturalist. If he spent half as much time as I did back here, the things he would know!"

The empty nest was so well-camouflaged it was difficult to detect. If the kids saw it, they'd probably notice its distinctive construction. The outside is made of coarse, dry grass; the hollow of the nest is lined with mud, and then a final layer of finer grass as a cushion for the eggs. The female robin is the one who sits on the eggs; unlike her flashy, orange-breasted mate, her colorings are more subdued—a natural adaptation to keep predators from noticing her while she sits on her eggs. The more one knows about the natural world, the more amazingly complex it becomes.

Underneath the same honeysuckle bush, I noticed what looked like opossum tracks in the damp soil. I have met these almost cartoon-like characters on many an evening trip to the trash barrel. The urban nature of their surroundings seems to suit them well; I mind their presence (what with their penchant for knocking over the trash barrel and discriminatively picking through its contents) much more than they seem to mind mine. But as much of a mess as they can make with your garbage, its still kind of a thrill to see a large, wild mammal come into your backyard.

Like the raccoon, the opossum sleeps during the day and comes out to feed at night. In the wild, the opossum favors hollow tree stumps for its nests. In cities and towns, it will take up residence almost anywhere—under a porch or deck, in a storm drain, or under the foundation of your house.

For the oldest surviving family of mammals, opossums have surprisingly small, primitive brains. The term "playing possum" comes from the way these not-so-bright animals deal with an intensely

Few backyard residents are more intriguing than fireflies. Their luminescent mystery has yet to be unraveled.

stressful situation, such as being trapped by a predator. They collapse on the ground, close their eyes, curl back their lips (imitating a very dead, dried opossum) often allowing their tongues to hang out of their mouths. Faced with this unappetizing sight, the predator, more often than not, retreats. In 10 to 20 minutes, the opossum snaps out of it and goes safely on its way.

Looking up from the opossum tracks, I noticed the first fireflies rising up off the lawn, as if the grass itself had come to life, each blade changing its color from merely green to phosphorescent brilliance as it hovered heavenward. Looking closer at the grass I saw baby crickets—lots of them—no more than a quarter-inch long. With my nose practically pressed against the lawn, I watched them flit from one tall head of clover to another.

Fireflies definitely fall under the heading of "unsolved mysteries." Technically speaking, they are beetles, not flies. They start life as grubs (or glowworms, because they glow even in the larval stage!) and are then transformed into the flying beetles we know as fireflies, lantern bugs, or lightening bugs. Scientists still do not know exactly how or why fireflies glow. It is a subject of scientific interest not only because the light is "cold" (it does not produce any measurable heat), but also because the fuel for the firefly's light, a substance called luciferin, is not used up as it is "burned." Who knows? Some day this mystery may be solved by a scientist who started out as a backyard naturalist.

Two houses over, a wind from the south rustled through an enormous old cottonwood tree. There are only two trees I know of, cottonwoods and quaking aspen, whose leaves respond to the slightest breeze. Each leaf twists and turns in a dizzying dance, like the sound of so much taffeta swirling around to a waltz. I didn't recall hearing the weather report call for rain, but the heavy rustle of that cottonwood tree almost always means that rain is not far behind. An old folk tale claims that the cross on which Jesus was crucified was made from cottonwood, and that ever since then the cottonwood tree has shuddered nervously.

I sat on the low stone wall and looked up at a gathering sky, listening to the towhees sing their melodic song—reliable chimes that announced evening was falling. And that wasn't all. Within five minutes of the cottonwood's weather prediction, big fat drops of rain began plopping down. Far off there was the sound of thunder. The cat jumped up from under the shrubbery and scurried back to the safety of the house. I was right behind him, more than satisfied with the findings of this short expedition.

The next day, I ordained the kids as official "backyard naturalists" and sent them on their mission, outfitted with bag lunches, paper, pencils, a magnifying glass, a net and collection jars, with the assurance that they would let the creatures free once they had observed them in detail.

Although I had recommended that they spend at least twenty minutes in the backyard, they stayed out there the entire afternoon, crawling and climbing about. When they finally came in, they reported on everything from three kinds of spider webs, a woodpecker eating insects as he walked up the bark of a tree, six different types of butterflies and moths, and three huge tomato hornworms. They found the abandoned robin's nest, and even the tracks of the opossum. In addition, they had dozens of questions, not all of which I could answer.

This led to an excursion to the library, where the kids were astounded by the number of interesting identification books that were available. Whether the day's activities lead to any of them becoming full-fledged naturalists is impossible to say, but I guarantee that they'll never view the backyard in quite the same way. And neither will I.

Gerald Durrell was right: "As a naturalist you will never suffer from that awful modern disease called boredom—so go out and greet the natural world with curiosity and delight."

"Twenty minutes he spends out here, and all of a sudden he's an expert. You gotta laugh."

BACKYARD DENIZENS

TO SOME, THEY'RE RODENTS WITH BUSHY TAILS. TO OTHERS, PLAYFUL CLOWNS TRIPPING FROM LIMB TO LIMB. THEIR MOST ANNOYING TRAIT MAY BE THE WAY THEY INGENIOUSLY ROB BIRD FEEDERS. SEE PAGES 122-123 FOR SOME SQUIRREL-PROOF BIRD FEEDERS—GUARANTEED!

THE COMMON CROW TENDS TO TRAVEL IN PACKS AND MAKE ITS PRESENCE KNOWN WITH ITS LOUD AND NOT ALTOGETHER PLEASANT CAW-CAW. THESE ARE BIG BIRDS, WITH BIG APPETITES, EATING A LOT OF INSECTS ALONG THE WAY.

NO, THEY WON'T COME ALONG AND SEW YOUR LIPS TOGETHER IF YOU TELL A LIE—HONEST. DRAGONFLIES ARE AMONG THE MOST INTERESTING OF FLYING INSECTS, HOVERING, DARTING, AND DASHING THIS WAY AND THAT. IT'S NOT AIMLESS WANDERING, HOWEVER: THEY EAT ON THE RUN— SNACKING ON OTHER INSECTS IN THE AIR, RATHER THAN ON THE GROUND.

THE LARGE, LUMBERING BUMBLEBEE PLODS FROM FLOWER TO FLOWER, GATHERING POLLEN ON ITS HIND LEGS AND DRINKING NECTAR WITH ITS LONG TONGUE. SO INTENT ON BUSINESS, IT WILL ONLY STING YOU IF YOU GO OUT OF YOUR WAY AND STEP ON IT.

THE GREEN ANOLE IS OFTEN CALLED A CHAMELEON BECAUSE OF ITS ABILITY TO CHANGE COLORS. AS AN INSECT EATER, IT SHOULD BE WELCOME IN ANY YARD.

THE INTRICATELY PAINTED BOX TURTLE IS CONTENT TO MUNCH DAINTILY ON INSECTS, BERRIES, AND THE LEAVES OF A FEW FAVORED PLANTS. THIS GENTLE SOUL CAN LIVE FOR AS LONG AS 30 YEARS.

IT'S AMAZING HOW MANY URBAN AND SUBURBAN YARDS PLAY HOST TO RABBITS. BUT, THEN AGAIN, GIVEN THEIR FERTILE HABITS, PERHAPS IT ISN'T. THEY FAVOR TALL, UNMOWN PLOTS OF GRASS AND WEEDS AND UNTRIMMED SHRUB BORDERS.

AMONG THE MOST COLORFUL OF ALL BIRDS, THE MALE NORTHERN CARDINAL IS A DASHING ADDITION TO ANY BACKYARD. ITS FAVORITE FOOD IS SUNFLOWER SEEDS. LET A FEW SUNFLOWERS GO TO SEED IN YOUR GARDEN, AND YOU MAY PLAY HOST TO A LARGE CONGREGATION OF THESE BEAUTIFUL BIRDS.

RACCOONS ARE EVEN MORE FEARLESS AND GREGARIOUS THAN THEIR FRIENDS, THE OPOSSUMS. THEY THINK NOTHING OF SORTING THROUGH YOUR OVERTURNED GARBAGE CAN AS YOU STAND THERE AND WATCH THEM.

OPOSSUMS ARE MEMBERS OF THE OLDEST LIVING FAMILY OF MAMMALS, DATING BACK OVER 70 MILLION YEARS. FOR ALL THEIR LONGEVITY, THEY AREN'T VERY INTELLIGENT, BUT THEY MUST KNOW SOMETHING IMPORTANT. THEY'LL EAT VIRTUALLY ANYTHING, LIVE ALMOST ANYWHERE, AND ARE AS AT HOME IN THE SUBURBS AS THEY ARE IN THE WILD.

THE HOMELY COMMON TOAD IS A FRIENDLY AND HELPFUL BACKYARD CITIZEN. WITH AN APPETITE FOR INSECTS AND A DESIRE TO BE LEFT ALONE IN COOL, DAMP RECESSES, THE TOAD IS A WELL-MANNERED MEMBER OF THE BACKYARD CLAN.

THE GREAT SPANGLED FRITILLARY IS A COMMON SIGHT IN MANY BACKYARD GARDENS. ALWAYS WELCOME VISITORS, BUTTERFLIES SEEM TO ADD A BIT OF FLOATING POETRY ON THE OTHERWISE INVISIBLE WIND.

THE FAMILIAR GARTER SNAKE IS A BIG EATER OF INSECTS AND SHOULD BE WELCOMED TO ANY BACKYARD. THAT'S NOT TO SAY, HOWEVER, THAT WHEN YOU UNEXPECTEDLY GREET ONE IN THE FLOWER BORDER, IT WILL BE A PLEASANT EXPERIENCE.

"Are you kidding? Some of these wild things are my closest friends. If you ever knew what went on after dark."

117

A Wildlife Sanctuary

A couple of years ago there was a movement to replace the typical front lawn with wild-looking "meadow" plantings. While there were sound environmental reasons for suggesting this type of landscaping, the few people bold enough to implement the meadow look found themselves at the receiving end of some rather strange looks from their neighbors.

The people who planted these meadow gardens noticed an increase in the number of birds, bees, butterflies, and other forms of wildlife visiting their front yards, but they were definitely bucking the tide and, in some cases, causing a political stir regarding an individual's right to non-conformity. More recently, most of these wildlife gardens have quietly moved from public to private, finding a more hospitable home in the backyard.

While other gardeners dream about planting a rose or vegetable garden, wildlife gardeners have visions of "butterfly gardens," or "winter bird gardens" in mind. This shift in emphasis produces gardens quite unlike anything you might expect in anyone's backyard—especially in the city or suburbs.

You may be wondering if it's really possible to create a miniature wildlife sanctuary in an urban or suburban backyard. The boundaries that homeowners put up around their yards don't mean a thing to most wildlife. To the bluebird or monarch butterfly flying overhead, the turtle plod-

A wildlife sanctuary—tame enough to be beautiful, wild enough to be fascinating.

ding his way through the grass, or the salamander slinking her way through the damp undergrowth, a backyard can be simply another bit of the environment in which they live. The reason we don't see more wildlife in our backyards is that most of us don't plant anything to attract them or create places for them to seek shelter. Once you do, you'll be amazed at how quickly wildlife will visit, and at how many take up permanent residence, in your backyard.

The few backyard wildlife gardens I have visited have been beautiful, intriguing places. In most of these backyards, the lawns had been eliminated. Gone, too, were the neatly trimmed shrub borders, replaced with informal plantings of annuals and perennials, with meandering walks covered with pine needles or bark. All of the wildlife gardens I have seen contained at least one small pool; a source of fresh water is essential to all forms of wildlife.

Owners of these gardens speak of them as acting like magnets. The sights and sounds of wildlife, as they dash and flit about the garden, pull the owners from their beds early enough for a morning stroll, even on those hurly-burly workdays. Sunlight streaming through at long angles, turning dewdrops on spider webs into delicate diamond necklaces, the whirring of the first hummingbird as it looks for a fresh flower, the languid movement of butterflies as they warm their wings in the morning light, and the plop of a frog as it jumps into the murky water work in concert, creating a peaceful note on which to start the day.

All gardens require upkeep, but informal gardens planted with attracting wildlife in mind are far less demanding than a more traditional backyard landscape. Plants can be allowed to find their natural forms instead of being trimmed into tidy shapes. A weed here or there isn't such an eyesore when it is growing amid a profusion of billowing plants. And if you choose to eliminate the lawn (which is *not* a prerequisite, I should point out), one major source of upkeep is also eliminated.

Even though the garden may be informal, be sure to define places to sit, relax, and take in the sights of your sanctuary. A wooden bench under a spreading tree, a couple of chaise lounges on a patio overlooking the pond, or a clearing in a grove of trees for a picnic table and benches will provide human comfort while you view your own private wildlife preserve.

Humans have a natural curiosity about the other living species with whom we share this planet. When wildlife can be seen up close—right outside your back door—the natural world and all its inhabitants become real, not just something seen in a book or at a zoo, commanding even greater respect and protection. And although your original intent may have been to create a sanctuary for wildlife, you may find that in the process you've created a sanctuary for yourself.

Gardening With Wildlife

Since 1973, The National Wildlife Federation in Washington, D.C., has been making information available to home owners interested in attracting wildlife to their gardens. Initial response was so strong, the federation actually created a do-it-yourself kit available to anyone interested in the subject. The Gardening With Wildlife Kit, which contains everything you need to plan a backyard wildlife habitat, sells for $29.95 (plus $3.95 shipping) and can be ordered from The National Wildlife Federation, 1400 16th Street NW, Washington, D. C. 20036-2266. Ask for item #79914.

As an additional incentive, the National Wildlife Federation will, on request, certify your garden. Upon certification, the federation will send you a certificate proclaiming your yard to be an official Backyard Wildlife Habitat of the National Wildlife Federation. Why not be the first on your block to display this certificate?

If there are youngsters in your household, this type of activity is one of the best ways to teach them the value of protecting and nurturing the environment. It's a project the whole family can benefit from, on a scale where results are almost immediate.

"I tell you, it's getting a little crowded around here. Any more wildlife, and I'm going next door."

AUGUST 28

Finally found the page
I've been looking for —
the last one! Time
to put the pen and
brush away and shout
hallelujah!

A.C.S.

*No matter what
you're celebrating,
the backyard is a
place to do it with
sheer abandonment.
Isn't that why you
built that fence?*

EPILOGUE

t is my sincere hope that the words and pictures in this book have inspired you to create your own backyard retreat.

I'd be lying, however, if I said that backyards don't require care and attention—they do. And at a time when so many are trying to simplify their lives, one more thing to take care of may be the last thing we think we need. Oddly, though, a backyard is that rare place that gives back far more than it requires.

As I sat in his backyard one day, an old man passed on his observations with regard to what he was convinced were the restorative qualities of outdoor work. "Tensions," he said in characteristic brevity, "flow down through the handle of a hoe" and added wryly that "a Sunday morning spent pulling weeds takes care of the excesses of a Saturday night." The chores demanded by backyards, it seems, come along with their own rewards.

I've watched people rush home from work, distracted and out of sorts, only to be transformed the moment they put a garden hose in their hand. As placid and relaxed as a human fountain, spraying water around the yard amid the lengthening shadows, I can say with certainty that the backyard is a restorative place...a place to ground one's self...a place to grow to your heart's content.

I'm sure that's what Voltaire meant when he ended the book *Candide* with the following advice: "We must cultivate our garden." By so doing, we may find the time and peace to cultivate our lives.

Just one last Thot: "z-z-z-z-z-z-z-z."

PRODUCT INDEX

Please note: Numbers correspond to mail-order sources listed at right. Information is current as of publication date.

Bird Baths
    General, 2, 3, 4, 6, 7, 8, 9, 15, 17, 19, 20, 23, 24
    Heated, 2, 3, 17
    Terra Cotta, 19
Bird Houses/Feeders
    Bat houses, 17
    Bluebird houses, 3
    General, 2, 3, 5, 6, 8, 9, 17, 24
    Hummingbird feeder, 2, 3
    Purple Martin houses, 2, 3, 17
    Seed, 3
    Squirrel-proof, 2, 3, 5, 9, 12, 17
    Thatched, 3, 19
    Wood-Crete, 12, 19
Constructed Items
    Arbors, 2, 6, 8, 9, 12, 19
    Bridges, 15, 19
    Gates, 19
    Gazebos, 6, 8, 15
    Playhouse kits, 9
    Trelliswork, treillage, 2, 8, 12
Containers
    Cast aluminum, 6
    Fiberglass, 8
    Planters, teak, 19
    Plastic, 6, 12
    Terra cotta, 6, 8, 15, 19
    Windowboxes, 19, 24
    Wooden, 6, 19
Fireplaces
    Portable outdoor, 9, 20
Flag Poles
    Free-standing, 1, 20
    Telescoping, 1, 2, 9, 20
    Wall-mounted, 1, 2, 17, 20
Flags
    American, 1, 2, 20
    Custom-designed, 1
    "Don't Tread on Me," 1, 20

    Historical, 1
    International, 1
    Japanese fish, 1
    Marine, 1
    State, 1, 20
Furniture
    Benches, 2, 6, 9, 19, 20
    Canopies, 6, 20
    Cast aluminum, 15
    Chairs, 2, 6, 9, 19, 20, 24
    Hammocks, 2, 5, 6, 8, 17, 19, 20
    Italian market, 18
    Metal, 19, 24
    Porch rockers, 8, 9, 19
    Rattan, 8
    Swings, 6, 8, 9, 17, 19, 20
    Tables, 2, 6, 8, 9, 19, 20, 24
    Teak, 8, 19
    Umbrellas, 2, 6, 8, 19
    Umbrellas, Italian market, 19
    Wicker, 8, 19, 24
    Willow, 8
    Wrought iron, 6, 8, 15, 19
Fountains
    Free-standing, 4, 24
    Heads, 6, 10, 13, 22
    Pond, 6, 8, 15
    Wall-mounted, 4, 6, 9, 19, 23
Games
    Basketball, 20
    Bocce, 5, 17, 20, 25
    Combination sets, 25
    Croquet, 5, 6, 17, 25
    French hoops, 25
    Handball, 5
    Horseshoes, 5, 9, 17, 20, 25
    Marbles, 25
    Pétanque, 25
    Polo, spongee, 25
    Volleyball, 5, 17, 25
    Water games, 6, 20
    Water slides, 6
Lighting
    Candles, 8
    Floodlights, 21

    General, 16, 20
    Halogen, 19
    Lanterns, general, 8, 15, 19, 24
    Lanterns, Chinese paper, 8
    Lanterns, hand-carved stone, 16
    Low voltage, 19
    Minispot, 21
    Path, 19, 21
    Security, 2, 21
    Solar, 2, 8, 19
    Stair and railing, 21
    Torches, 8
Natural Controls
    Lawn Controls, 18
    Pest Controls, 18
    Rose Controls, 18
Ornament
    Bells, garden, 7, 8, 26, 28, 23
    Gazing balls, 4, 14
    Lanterns, hand-carved stone, 16
    Statuary, 2, 4, 6, 7, 8, 9, 15, 24
    Sundials, 2, 5, 6, 7, 9, 15, 20, 23, 24
    Wall plaques, 4, 9, 15, 17, 24
    Weather vanes, 6, 8, 9, 17, 23
    Wind chimes, 6, 7, 8, 9, 17, 19, 23, 24
Recycling/Composting Supplies
    Compost bins, 2, 5, 6, 8, 9, 12, 17, 18, 19
    Recycling cabinets, 2
    Recycling centers, 5, 8, 9, 17
Water Gardening
    Basins, 16
    Bog plants, 10, 13, 22
    Fish, 13, 22
    Fish bowls, Chinese porcelain, 6, 8
    Fish care supplies, 10, 13, 22
    Filters, 10, 13, 22
    Liners, 10, 13, 22
    Pumps, 10, 13, 22
    Tub gardens, 13, 22
    Underwater lights, 13, 22
    Water plants, 10, 13, 22
    Waterfalls, 22

PRODUCT SOURCES

1. All Nations Flag Co., Inc.
   118 W. 5th Street
   Kansas City, MO 64105
   1-800-533-FLAG

2. Alsto's Handy Helpers
   PO Box 1267
   Galesburg, IL 61401
   1-800-447-0048

3. Audubon Workshop
   1501 Paddock Drive
   Northbrook, IL 60062
   1-800-325-9464

4. Ballard Designs
   1670 DeFoor Avenue N.W.
   Atlanta, GA 30318-7528
   (404) 351-5099

5. Brookstone
   5 Vose Farm Road
   Peterborough, NH 03458
   1-800-926-7000

6. David Kay
   4509 Taylor Lane
   Cleveland, OH 44128
   1-800-872-5588

7. Flora & Fauna
   38001 Old Stage Road
   Gualala, CA 95445-9984
   1-800-358-9120

8. Gardener's Eden
   PO Box 7307
   San Francisco, CA 94120
   1-800-822-9600

9. John Deere Catalog
   1400 Third Avenue
   Moline, IL 61265
   1-800-544-2122

10. Gilberg Perennial Farms
    2906 Ossenfort Road
    Glencoe, MO 63038
    (314) 458-2033

11. House of Tyrol
    PO Box 909
    Cleveland, GA 30528
    1-800-241-5404

12. The Kinsman Company
    River Road
    Point Pleasant, PA 18950
    1-800-733-5613

13. Lilypons Water Gardens
    6800 Lilypons Road
    Buckeystown, MD 21717-0010
    (301) 874-2959

14. Milaeger's Gardens
    4838 Douglas Avenue
    Racine, WI 53402-2498
    1-800-325-0305

15. Nightengale's Garden Co.
    29 Westgrove Lane
    London SE10 8QP
    01-692-1639

16. Phillip Hawk & Company
    159 East College Avenue
    Pleasant Gap, PA 16823
    (814) 355-7177

17. Plow & Hearth
    301 Madison Road
    Orange, VA 22960-0492
    1-800-627-1712

18. Ringer Corp.
    9959 Valley View Road
    Eden Prairie, MN 55344
    1-800-654-1047

19. Smith & Hawken
    25 Corte Madera
    Mill Valley, CA 94941
    (415) 383-2000

20. Sporty's
    Clermont County Airport
    Batavia, OH 45103-9747
    1-800-543-8633

21. Toro
    8500 Normandale Lake
    Minneapolis, MN 55437
    (612) 888-8801

22. Van Ness Water Gardens
    2460 North Euclid Avenue
    Upland, CA 91786-1199
    (714) 982-2425

23. Wind & Weather
    Albion Street Water Tower
    Mendocino, CA 95640
    1-800-922-9463

24. Winterthur
    100 Enterprise Place
    Dover, DE 19901
    1-800-767-0500

25. World Wide Games
    PO Box 517
    Colchester CT 06415-0517
    1-800-243-9232

INDEX

A

Adirondack chairs, **60**, **61**
All-purpose marinade, **101**
Anoles, **116**
Arbors, 29, 37, 38, 43, 96, 97
Autumnal Equinox, 73, 78
Awnings, **36**

B

Backyard naturalist, 111, 112, **114**, 115
Backyard Olympics, 76, 86, 87
Backyard scrapbook, **22**, 23, 26
Backyard walkabout, 24
Badminton, 88, 89
Bailey, Liberty Hyde, 49
Belvederes, 38
Benches, 35, **61**
Bentgrass, 16
Birds
    Birdbaths, 51, **53**, 56, 64
    Birdhouses, **69**
    Blackbirds, 113
    Cardinals, **117**
    Chimney swifts, 113
    Crows, **116**
    Feeding of, 83
    Grackles, 113
    Robins, 113, 114
Blue Moon, 79
Bocce, 88, 90
Boccie. *See* Bocce
Bog plants, 52
Bonfires, 79, 80
Boules. *See* Bocce
Bradford, William, 80, 81
Bruschetta, **101**
Building designers, 26
Bumblebees, **116**
Butterflies, **117**
Butterfly gardens, 118

C

Camping, backyard, 103, 108
Candide, 121
Carnivals, backyard, 103
Carpenter, 26
Carruth, George, 28
Catnip, **53**

Ceiling fans, 98
Chairs, 60, **61**
Chinese lanterns, **62**, 76
Church, Thomas, 17, 97
Citronella candles, 97
Clay pots, **67**
Compost, 46
Construction contractors, 26
Container plants, 57
Containers, 66, **67**
Cool food, **100**, **101**
Cost estimates, 26
Crabgrass, 49
Croquet, 16, 82, 88
cummings, e. e., 83
Cut flowers, 54
    When to cut, 55
Cutting gardens, 50, **54**

D

Dandelions, **48**, 49
Dean, Ruth, 96
Decks, 29, **34**, **35**, 42, 97
    Aprons, 35
    Free-standing, 34
    Japanese, 34
    Kits, **34**
    Unpainted wood, 35
Dipping wells, 51
Dog carts, 106
Dogs, **68**, 106, 108
Doorbells, 33
Dovecotes, **69**
Dragonflies, **116**
Duke of Suffolk, 87
Duncan, Frances, 15
Duncan, Isadora, 76
Durrell, Gerald, 111, 115

E

Easter, 72
    Easter egg hunt, 72
    Easter eve, 73
    Living Easter baskets, 72
Eye-catchers, 39, 52

F

Father's Day, 74, 86

Fences, 29, **30**, 31, 32
    Board-and-rail, **32**
    Dog-eared, **30**, 32
    Japanese, **30**
    Lattice, **30**
    Make-believe, **31**
    Picket, **30**
    Wrought-iron, **32**
Fertilizer, 46, 56, 57
Fire pits, 75, 77, 80
Fireflies, 114, 107
Fish
    Bowls, Japanese ceramic, **41**
    Goldfish, **14**, 51, 52
    Koi, **14**, 15, 51, 52
    Ponds, 15, 51
Flags, 64, 105
Flashlight, 98, 107, 108
Flashlight Hide-and-Seek, 85, 107
Flora, 73
Flower Moon, 79
Follies, 39
Forts, 42, 103, 109
Fountains, 51
    Wall, **50**, 51
Fourth of July, 74, 76
Full moons, names, 79
Furniture, 60, **61**

G

Games, 76, 85, 86, 91
    Improvising, 86
    Rules and regulations, 85
Gardens
    Cloistered, 53
    Cutting, 50, **54**
    Herb, 50
    Hobby, 50
    Kitchen, 50, **52**, 53
    Old-fashioned, 52
    Rose, 50, 55, **56**
    Secret, **24**
    Vegetable, 52, 53
    Water, 50, 51, 52
Garter snakes, **117**
Gates, 32
    Backyard, 32
    Board-and-rail, **32**
    Front, 32
    Lattice, **32**

See-through, 32
Side yard, 32
Solid wood, **32**, **33**
Victorian, **32**
Gazebos, **38**, 39, 40
Gazing balls, 53, 64, **65**
Geraniums, **66**
Goldfish, 52
Grape arbor, 96
Grilled chicken, **100**
Grilled flank steak, **100**
Grilled ratatouille, **101**
Grilled shrimp, **100**
Ground-breaking ceremony, 27
Groundcover, 48

H

Halloween, 79, 80
Hammocks, **35**, 60, **69**
Hardscape, 29, 30
Harvest Home, 81, 82
Hedges, 30, 31
Herb gardens, 50, **53**
Herbicides, 49
Hicks, David, 21
Hobby gardens, 50
Cutting gardens, 50, **54**
Herb gardens, 50
Kitchen gardens, 50, **52**, 53
Rose gardens, 50, 55,**56**
Water gardens, 50, 51, 52
Holidays, 71, 74
Hurricane lamps, **63**

I

Igloos, **82**
Indian Summer, 80
Insects, 49, 56
Natural pest controls, 49

J

Japanese fences, **30**
Japanese Festival of Spring, 72
Jekyll, Gertrude, 29, 30

K

Kitchen gardens, 50, **52**, 53
Koi, 14, 15, 51, 52

L

Labor Day, 74, 76, 77
Landscape architects, 26, 27
Landscape contractors, 26, 27
Landscape designers, 26, 27
Landscape, natural, 30
Landscaping, 17, 27
Lanterns, **63**, 108
Lattice
Fences, **30**, **32**
Gates, **32**
Overheads, **36**, **37**
peep-hole covers, 33
Pre-made panels, 43
Lawn bowls, 87
Lawn care
Clippings, **48**
Cutting, **48**
Natural controls, **48**
Natural fertilizers, **48**
Organic pesticides, 49
Seeding, **48**
Sodding, **48**
Watering, **48**
Weeds, **48**
Lawns, 47, 48
Lewis, C. S., 111
Lighting, 62, **63**
Chinese lanterns, 62
Installation of, 62
Kits, 62
Low-voltage systems, 62
Luminaries, 62
Midwestern party lights, 63
Modular systems, 62
Lime, 46
Lot line, 24
Luminaries, 62, **63**
Lutyens, Sir Edwin, 29, 30

M

Marbles, 92
Massasoit, 81
Matschat, Cecile, 64
May Day, 72, 73, 74, 75
May baskets, 74
Maypole dance, 74
Meadow plantings, 118
Memorial Day, 76

Metal furniture, 60
Midsummer's Night, 74, 75
Midwestern party lights, **63**
Model trains, 15, **16**
Monkey bars, 109
Moon, names of full moons, 79
Mosquitos, 96, 97, 98
Mosquito nets, **69**
Myers, Robert, 81

N

Natural controls
Lawn care, 48
Organic pesticides, 49
Natural landscape, 30
Natural plantings, 52
Naturalists, 111, 112, **114**, 115
Durrell, Gerald, 111, 115
Supplies, **112**

O

One-Act Plays, 15, 109
Opossums, 114, **117**
Organic matter, 46
Ornament, 64, **65**
Osiris, 72
Outbuildings, **40**, 42
Outdoor cook, 98
Outdoor cupboard, 98
Outdoor dining, 34, 96
Outdoor flooring, 97
Asphalt, 36
Brick, 36, 97
Concrete, 36, 97
Flagstone, 36, 97
Outdoor food, 99
Overheads, **36**, **37**
Awnings, **36**, 37
Corrugated fiberglass, 37
Free-standing, **36**
Lath, 37
Lattice, **36**, 37
Shade trees, 37
Solid roof, 98
Solid wood, **36**

P

Page, Russell, 17
Pandora's Turkey, 81

Parrish, Maxfield, 76
Passover, 72
Patios, 29
Pea gravel, 97
Peep-holes, **33**, **65**, **68**
    Heat register covers, 33, **65**
    Lattice, 33
    Oriental tiles, 33
Pergolas, 37, 38
Picket Fences, **30**
Plan, 23, 25, 26
Planning process, 20, 21, **44**
Planting plans, 47
Plants
    Bog, 52
    Common, 45
    Container, 57
    Experimental plantings, 49
    Hard-to-grow, 49
    High-maintenance, 50
    Low-maintenance, 50
    Rare, 45
    Selection of, 45, 47
    Watering, 57
Play Structures, 109
Plays
    One-act, 15, 109
    Outdoor, **16**, 107
Ponds, 51
    Fish, 15, 51
    Formal, **50**
    Naturalistic-looking, **50**
Pools
    Custom-designed, 51
    Electric heaters, 52
    Formal, 51
    Natural, 51, 52
    Vinyl liners, 51
Posts
    Brick, 34
    Gate, 33
Potagers, 53
Potpourri, 55
Pruning, 47, 56

R

Rabbits, **116**
Raccoons, 114, **117**, 52
Railings, 35
Ratatouille, **101**
Robin Hood, 73

Rose gardens, 50, 55, **56**
Roses, 55
    Bouquets, **56**
    Disease problems, 56, 57
    The Combined Rose List, 55
    Specific needs, 56

S

Sandboxes, 39, 41
Seasons, change of, 73
Secret gardens, **24**
Secret retreats, **39**, **40**, **42**, 43
Security systems, 33
Shade trees, **37**, 47, 50
Shakespeare, William, 109
Sheds, 42, 43
Shuffleboard, 92
Shuttlecock, **89**
Skewered beef, lamb, or pork, **100**
Slides, 109
Snow forts, **82**
Soil preparation, 46, 47, 54, 56
Soil testing, 56
Spool tractor, 106
Squirrels, **116**
Stain, 35, 36
Stairs, 35
Standish, Captain Miles, 81
Statuary, 64
Stone lanterns, **63**
Stool ball, 81
Summer Solstice, 73
Sunbathing, 34
Sundials, 53, 56, 64, **69**
Sunflower Lottery Party, 77
Swings, 16, 106, 109

T

Tables, 60, **61**
Terra cotta pots, 66, **67**
Terraces, 29
Thanksgiving, 80, 82
Tilework, 64
Tin-can telephones, 106
Toads, **117**
Togas, 76
Towhees, 115
Tree houses, 16, 39, **40**, 41
Trees
    Cottonwood, 114

Japanese elm, 42
    Shade, **37**, 47, 50
Treillage, 64
Trolls, 64, **65**
Turtles, **116**

U

Umbrellas, **38**, 60, **61**
Urns, **67**

V

van der Rohe, Mies, 59
Vegetable pot luck, 79
Vegetable cleaning station, 52
Vernal Equinox, 73
Vining plants, 37, 38, 43
Volleyball, 93
Voltaire, 121

W

Walkways, 29
Wall planters, **65**
Wall plaques, 64, **65**
Walls, 29, 30, 31
Water gardens, **50**, 51, 52
Water plants, 52
Watering, **48**, 56, 57
Weather vanes, **65**
Weeds, 48, 49
Wheelbarrows, 64
Whimsy, **69**
Wicker furniture, 60
Wilde, Oscar, 55
Wildlife, **116**, **117**, 83
    Gardening With Wildlife Kit, 119
    National Wildlife Federation, 119
    Wildlife Sanctuary, 118
Wind chimes, **69**
Windowboxes, 66, **67**
Winter Bird Gardens, 118
Winter Solstice, 73
Witches' balls, 64
Wolfe, Thomas, 21
Wooden containers, **67**
Wreaths, 79
Wrought-iron furniture, 60

Y

Yoch, Florence, 45, 51

About this Book

The body text of this book is set in Adobe Garamond Regular. The sidebars and captions are set in Adobe Garamond Italic. The illustration notes are set in a modified hand-lettered typeface called Tekton. *In Your Own Backyard* was designed and composed on a Macintosh computer system.

"Thot" is a flipbook. Flip back and see!

The Author Notes:

After spending 15 years writing a number of gardening books and being the editor of a national gardening magazine, I came to the conclusion that for every person who enjoys gardening, there are probably ten who simply enjoy being outdoors—but don't want to leave home in order to do it. This book was written for all of those non-gardening, outdoor-loving people. I hope you enjoy it.

I grew up in California's Napa Valley, attended the University of California at Berkeley. I now live in Kansas City, with my wife and 12-year-old daughter. It's a town with a lot of wonderful backyards and friendly people. I've been influenced by both.

A. Cort Sinnes